DK EYEWITNESS TRAVEL

TOP

MADEIRA

CHRISTOPHER CATLING

D0483767

Penguin
Random
House

Top 10 Madeira Highlights

The Top 10 of Everything

CONTENTS

Madeira Area by Area

Streetsmart

Within each Top 10 list in this book, no hierarchy of quality or popularity is implied. All 10 are, in the editor's opinion, of roughly equal merit.

Front cover and spine View at Cabo Girão, Madeira's highest cliff, in Camara de Lobos village, Madeira
Back cover Aerial view of Camara de Lobos village, Madeira
Title page Formal garden display in Madeira's botanical gardens, Funchal

Welcome to
Madeira

A place of mountain grandeur painted in vivid colours, sun-soaked Madeira lies in a clear blue Atlantic Ocean. This subtropical island is a scenic masterpiece. It is a culturally rich destination that is steeped in tradition, and visitors warm to its welcoming character. With Eyewitness Top 10 Madeira, it is yours to explore.

Madeira enjoys year-round appeal. It is celebrated for its world-famous wines, beautiful parks and gardens and an interior etched with an extraordinary network of *levada* footpaths.

Lively Funchal is built around centuries of history: its lovely **cathedral** dates from the 16th century and there are fabulous Flemish artworks in the **Museu de Arte Sacra**. Linger in **Museu da Quinta das Cruzes**, the home of João Gonçalves Zarco, who claimed Madeira for Portugal in 1420. Wander the **Zona Velha** (Old Town), now full of funky bars, hip galleries and quirky eateries. Luxury properties and Michelin-starred restaurants characterize Funchal's modern Hotel Zone.

Away from the city, Madeira is a top outdoors destination. The walking and hiking is among the best in Europe, with some trails crowning the island's highest peaks and others snaking through the UNESCO-listed *laurissilva* **forest**. Warm, crystal blue waters offer watersports opportunities, and whale- and dolphin-watching trips are truly memorable. Neighbouring **Porto Santo** is worth a detour, not least for its magnificent golden sandy beach.

Whether you're visiting for a weekend or a week, our Top 10 guide brings together the best of everything Madeira has to offer. There are useful tips throughout, from seeking out what's free to avoiding the crowds, plus seven easy-to-follow itineraries, designed to tie together a clutch of sights in a short space of time. Add inspiring photography and detailed maps, and you've got the essential pocket-sized travel companion. **Enjoy the book, and enjoy Madeira.**

Clockwise from top: **The castle of Sao Tiago**, vintage Portugese tile, Madeiran church, **flowers overlooking the water**, local flower, levada trails, beach in Madeira

Exploring Madeira

A destination of beauty with a mild climate, this exotic island captivates with its cultural richness and exuberant landscape. Here are ideas for a two- and seven-day stay, to help you discover the island's vibrant capital, dramatic coastline and spectacular mountain scenery.

Inside Funchal Cathedral there is an ornate 16th-century altarpiece.

Two Days in Funchal

Day ❶

MORNING

Learn about the island's history at the **Madeira Film Experience** *(see p76)* and take a guided walking tour with **History Tellers** *(see p76)*. Kick off the sightseeing in style at the glitzy **Museu CR7** *(see p59)* and then allow at least an hour to browse the magnificent art collection at **Museu de Arte Sacra** *(see pp14–15)*.

AFTERNOON

After lunch, enjoy the exhibits at the **Museu da Quinta das Cruzes** *(see pp18–21)* before visiting **Funchal Cathedral (Sé)** *(see pp12–13)*. End the day with a pre-booked guided tour of **Blandy's Wine Lodge** *(see pp16–17)*.

Day ❷

MORNING

Join the throngs at **Mercado dos Lavradores** *(see pp24–5)*. Next, be enlightened at **Casa da Luz – Museu de Electricidade** *(see p22)*. Spend the rest of the morning absorbing the information at the fascinating **Madeira Story Centre** *(see p23)*.

AFTERNOON

Continue exploring **Zona Velha** *(see pp22–5)* and shop at **Armazém do Mercado** *(see p23)*. Finish the day by scrambling over the 17th-century **Fortaleza de São Tiago** *(see p22)* and dinner at **Gavião Novo** *(see p79)*.

Seven Days in Madeira

Days ❶ and ❷

Follow the two-day Funchal itinerary.

Day ❸

Take the cable car to **Jardim Botânico** *(see pp26–9)* via **Monte** *(see pp34–5)*. Return from Monte by a thrilling toboggan ride back into town. Later, head to the **marina** *(see p75)* for a sightseeing cruise or **whale- and dolphin-watching excursion** *(see p58)*.

Day ❹

Drive to **Pico do Arieiro** *(see pp38–9)* for spectacular mountain views. Double back to **Ribeiro Frio** *(see p83)* for lunch at the restaurant. Walk off the

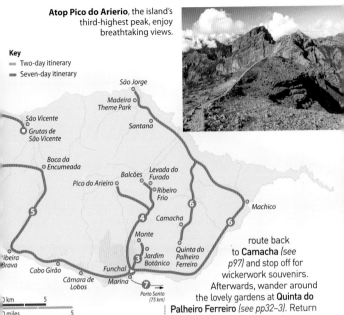

Atop Pico do Arieiro, the island's third-highest peak, enjoy breathtaking views.

Key
— Two-day itinerary
— Seven-day itinerary

São Jorge

Madeira Theme Park

São Vicente

Grutas de São Vicente

Santana

Boca da Encumeada

Balcões

Levada do Furado

Pico do Arieiro

Ribeiro Frio

Machico

Camacha

Monte

Quinta do Palheiro Ferreiro

Jardim Botânico

Ribeira Brava

Cabo Girão

Câmara de Lobos

Funchal

Marina

Porto Santo (75 km)

0 km   5
0 miles   5

meal by following the **Levada do Furado** (see p55) to Balcões for fabulous valley views. Dine in Funchal at **Armazém do Sal** (see p79).

Day ❺
Arrive early at **Câmara de Lobos** (see p82). Marvel at the dizzying panorama from **Cabo Girão** (see p81). From **Ribeira Brava** (see p87) head inland to **Boca da Encumeada** (see p81) and take the Paúl da Serra road to **Porto Moniz** (see p88) and a lovely restaurant, **O Cachalote** (see p91). Head east to **São Vicente** (see p87) and the wonderfully evocative **Grutas de São Vicente** (see p58) before heading back.

Day ❻
Breakfast in **Machico** (see p95) and, if it's open, visit the **Capela dos Milagres** (see p47). In Santana find the iconic A-frame houses (see p82). Admire sea vistas at **São Jorge** (see p54) before visiting the family-friendly **Madeira Theme Park** (see p58). In the afternoon, opt for the scenic

route back to **Camacha** (see p97) and stop off for wickerwork souvenirs. Afterwards, wander around the lovely gardens at **Quinta do Palheiro Ferreiro** (see pp32–3). Return to Funchal to ponder the day over a delicious dinner made with local ingredients at **Dona Amelia** (see p79).

Day ❼
Embark on a leisurely day cruise to Porto Santo. In **Vila Baleira** (see p101), visit the **Casa Museu Cristóvão Colombo** (see p102). Afterwards, relax over refreshments at one of the cafés in Largo do Pelourinho. If the day is hot and sunny, head to the beach (see p52). If you'd rather explore, hire a scooter and follow the **Porto Santo itinerary** (see p103). Arrive back at Vila Baleira in time for the return cruise to Funchal.

Porto Santo beach is a glorious expanse of golden sand, ideal for sunbathing.

Top 10 Madeira Highlights

Volcanic mountain scenery, as seen
from the Pico de Arieiro

🔟 Madeira Highlights

Madeira is an island of contrasts: the sophistication of the capital, Funchal, compared with the primeval woodland that cloaks the island's interior, and the fertile, flower-filled gardens with the arid volcanic peaks. There are also the gently rippling *levadas* (canals), and the crashing waves that dash the island's rocky shores.

1 Funchal Cathedral (Sé)

Hewn out of the island's rock and timber, Madeira's cathedral is a monument to the piety of the island's first settlers *(see pp12–13)*.

2 Museu de Arte Sacra, Funchal

Trade contacts with Antwerp in the 15th century enabled Madeira's merchants to sell their valuable sugar and buy the Flemish works of art that fill this museum *(see pp14–15)*.

3 Blandy's Wine Lodge, Funchal

Madeira is renowned for its wines, famous for their complexity and depth of flavour. At this historic wine lodge, you can learn to be a Madeira connoisseur *(see pp16–17)*.

4 Museu da Quinta das Cruzes, Funchal

Look inside a gracious Madeiran mansion, built on the site of the home of the island's first ruler, João Gonçalves Zarco *(see pp18–21)*.

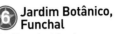

5 Zona Velha
Funchal's Old Town is the city's hippest nightlife hub: a collection of lively bars and talked-about restaurants around Rua de Santa Maria (see pp22–5).

6 Jardim Botânico, Funchal
The Botanical Gardens are a great showcase for the plants that thrive in the island's warm and humid climate, from orchids to cacti (see pp26–9).

7 Quinta do Palheiro Ferreiro
Two centuries of cultivation have produced this lovely all-seasons garden where the flowers of the world blend with the English flair for garden design (see pp32–3).

8 Monte
Escape to a romantic world of gardens and teahouses at this home of Emperor Charles I in exile. Return on the Monte toboggan run (see pp34–5).

9 Curral das Freiras
During pirate attacks, the nuns of Santa Clara took refuge in this hidden valley encircled by sheer cliffs – a place of breathtaking beauty (see pp36–7).

10 Pico do Arieiro
Feel on top of the world as you view the island's rugged, mountainous interior from the summit of Madeira's third-highest peak (see pp38–9).

TOP 10 ⭐ Funchal Cathedral (Sé)

Save for a flurry of pinnacles at the eastern end, Funchal Cathedral's exterior is very plain. By contrast, the interior is lined with statues, paintings and gold-covered chapels; the ceiling is comprised of spectacular knotwork inspired by Moorish geometry; and set in the floor are the tombs of early bishops and sugar merchants. Designed by Pêro Anes, assisted by master mason Gil Enes, the cathedral was begun in 1493. Consecrated in September 1514, when Funchal was officially granted city status, it was finally completed in October 1517.

NEED TO KNOW

MAP P3 ■ Largo da Sé
■ 291 228 155

Open 9am–noon & 4–6pm daily

■ The cathedral marks the city's social heart. The pavement cafés to the south (Funchal and Apolo) are popular meeting spots for those who live and work in the centre, and great places to relax and watch the world go by.

■ The cathedral is a functioning religious building, and visits are not encouraged during services (weekdays at 8am, 8:30am, 11:15am and 6pm; Sundays at 8am, 9am, 11am, 5pm and 6:15pm). If you wish to attend a service, you will have the opportunity to see the normally dark interior of the church lit up.

1 South Transept

Sunlight floods through the transept windows to light up the timber ceiling with its everlasting knots making arabesques and stars **(right)**. Faded figures around the edge of the ceiling depict Fortune holding a billowing sail, centaurs and fish-tailed mermen.

2 North Aisle

Madeira's trade links with Antwerp are reflected in an unusual 16th-century brass memorial set in the floor to the west of the first chapel. The brass shows the merchant Pedro de Brito Oliveira Pestana and his wife Catarina.

3 Baptistry

The vestibule to the church is paved in worn, 16th-century tomb slabs of black basalt. A wall plaque records the visit of Pope John Paul II on 12 May 1991. To the left is the massive 16th-century font of the Gothic baptistry.

4 Seating in the Sanctuary

Carved in 1510–11, and attributed to Flemish sculptor Olivier de Gand, the bold blue-and-gold choir stalls **(left)** depict saints, the Apostles and prophets dressed in the elaborate attire of merchants.

7 West Portal

King Manuel I of Portugal (1495–1521) helped to fund the construction of the cathedral, and therefore it is his coat of arms that appears over the Gothic doorway **(left)**. The delicate rose window set above the small crown is carved out of the rust-red local basalt.

KNOTWORK CEILINGS

Funchal Cathedral has one of the richest and most elaborate of Portuguese knotwork ceilings, comparable in splendour to the ceiling of the Chapel of the Royal Palace at Sintra. Funchal's delirious and dizzying pattern of knots and lozenges, with projections similar to stalactites, is based on the rich geometric art of medieval Islam. Much of Portugal was under Moorish rule from AD 711 to AD 1249.

---

9 East End

Go outside to the east end for the best view of the spire, and for the bravado display of barley-sugar pinnacles and pierced balustrades.

10 Sanctuary

The nautical theme continues on the gilded ceiling of the sanctuary, where a carving of an armillary sphere (a navigation aid) is among the painted cherubs and floral swags.

5 Altarpiece

The sizeable altarpiece **(above)** was made in the early 16th century. Set within its ornate Gothic frames are 12 scenes from the lives of Christ and the Virgin.

6 Nave and South Aisle

In this area **(right)**, there are many floor memorials to bishops and merchants. Carved in marble and basalt, they reflect the 16th-century Portuguese style.

8 Ceiling

Madeira's native white cedar trees were used to brilliant effect in the construction of the ceiling of the nave, aisles and transepts. It is one of the finest examples in Portugal of *alfarge*, or "knotwork", a technique blending Moorish and European elements.

TOP 10 ⭐ Museu de Arte Sacra, Funchal

Madeira is not the first place you would think of to look for some of the finest Flemish masterpieces, but the 15th-century sugar trade between Funchal and Antwerp (in modern Belgium) provides the link. Merchants and plantation owners commissioned altarpieces showing themselves and their families. Thus the colourful paintings in this museum of religious art are also portraits of some of the first settlers.

1 St Philip and St James by Pieter Coecke van Aelst

Here (above), the donors, pictured kneeling either side of the central panel, are Simão Gonçalves de Câmara, grandson of Zarco, and his wife Isabel.

2 Processional Cross

This exquisite silverwork (right) was donated at the dedication of Funchal's cathedral in 1514 by King Manuel I of Portugal (1495–1521). Gothic niches are filled with tiny figures of saints and scenes from the Passion and Crucifixion.

3 Entrance Hall

The importance of the bishop in local life is reflected in his elegant palace, which is now the museum. Visitors enter via a handsome hall floored with pebbles forming swags and garlands. A Baroque stone staircase, from the 1750s, is flanked by gilded candelabra.

4 The Machico Adoration

This anonymous painting of around 1518 from the church at Machico (see p95) depicts in detail Madeiran merchants and landowners in the guise of the Three Kings.

5 Annunciation by Joost van Cleve

The fruits of Europe's expanding trade connections can be seen in this serene painting of around 1515: Mary's feet rest on an oriental carpet, and the lilies symbolizing her purity stand in a Delft jar.

6 The Last Supper Tableau

This almost life-size wooden tableau **(above)** was carved for the cathedral in 1648 by Manuel Pereira. Judas sits alone clutching a money bag.

7 St Sebastian

This painted stone statue **(below)**, carved by Diogo Pires in the early 16th-century, is full of holes that once held arrows. St Sebastian, the Roman martyr, was condemned to death for his faith. He survived the arrows, but was later beheaded.

8 Deposition by Gerard David

The Virgin's face **(below)** shows resignation in the central panel of this triptych of 1518. Side panels depict Simon Acciaiuoli, a merchant from Florence (with St Bernardino of Siena), and his wife Maria (with St James) – the donors.

9 St James by Dieric Bouts

A study of St James, probably painted in Bruges in the 1470s, shows the saint's scarlet cloak. This and the flower-filled meadow in which he stands are typical of Flemish master Dieric Bouts' colour and naturalistic detail.

10 St Anne and St Joachim

This fascinating early 16th-century painting of the Antwerp School **(right)** is said to show King Ladislaw III of Poland *(see p43)* and his wife Senhorina Eanes. Portuguese tradition has it that the king gave up his crown after the Battle of Varna and settled on Madeira in 1454, where he was known as Henry the German.

FLEMISH ART

Madeiran art patrons would probably not have visited Antwerp or Bruges to sit for their portraits. Instead, they might have sent a sketch (perhaps drawn by one of the island's architects or masons) or perhaps relied on a friend to give the artist an accurate verbal description. In any case, creating an exact likeness was not the artist's aim. Following the Mannerist tendency, the painter of the Machico *Adoration* emphasizes distinctive facial features – a large nose, a double chin, a prominent forehead – in order to give character to his subjects.

NEED TO KNOW

MAP P3 ▪ Rua do Bispo 21 ▪ 291 228 900 ▪ www. museuartesacrafunchal. org

Open 10am–12:30pm & 2:30–5pm Tue–Sat, 10am–1pm Sun

Adm €3

▪ The Renaissance loggia facing onto Praça do Município is now the chic Café do Museu. A great place for a snack, lunch or early evening meal, the café serves salads, pasta dishes, homemade soups and light meals from 10am to 7:30pm.

TOP 10 ⭐ Blandy's Wine Lodge, Funchal

With its heavy ancient beams and cobblestone courtyards, Blandy's Wine Lodge can provide a solid introduction to the history of its unique wine. It is set in the surviving parts of a 17th-century Franciscan friary, most of which was demolished when Portugal passed its laws banning religious orders in 1834. The premises were acquired by the Blandy family in 1840 and have been used ever since for making Madeira wine.

NEED TO KNOW

MAP P3 ■ Avenida Arriaga 28 ■ 291 228 978 ■ www.blandyswine lodge.com

Open 10am–6:30pm Mon–Fri, 10am–1pm Sat

Premium Tour: 10:30am, 2:30pm, 3:30pm & 4:30pm Mon–Fri, 11am Sat; €5.90; Vintage Tour: 4:30pm Mon–Fri; €16.50

■ To the west of the wine lodge, there is an outdoor café located in the cloister of the São Francisco friary, now a lovely public garden.

■ You can enter the wine lodge anytime it is open. Wines may be sampled in the Max Römer Tasting Bar, and all the wines, including vintages, are payable by the glass. The cost is refundable when you buy a bottle of wine (except for vintage and package tours).

1 Max Römer Tasting Bar

The lovely sunny murals **(above)** of grape-growing and harvesting that cover the walls of the tasting bar on the ground floor were painted in 1922 by the German artist Max Römer (1878–1960).

2 Attics

Massive timbers support three storeys of ventilated attics. Wines here are aged in casks warmed only by the sun, a method known as *canteiro* that is used to produce quality wines.

Vintage Room 3

Within the Vintage Room **(right)**, precious wines are stored by date and kept behind bars. Madeira wines dating back to the early 20th century can be sampled here. Or it may be worth trying more moderately priced, but still appealing, vintages from the 1980s.

4 Courtyard

The romantic inner courtyard of the wine lodge is shaded by some of the island's tallest banana trees **(above)**. It is ringed by three storeys of attics with wisteria-draped balconies.

7 Wine Museum

Framed letters of appreciation from kings and queens, emperors, presidents and prime ministers – all lovers of Madeira wine – line the walls of the museum at the heart of the lodge. Also on display here are leather-bound ledgers **(left)** recording sales as far back as the 1700s.

MADEIRA WINE

Madeira wine has two defining characteristics. First, it is "fortified" by the addition of brandy at the final stage of the fermentation process. Second, it is heated as it ages in a process known as *estufagem (see p63)*. The benefits of heating were discovered when wines left on board ship after a round trip to the equator were found to have developed a new depth and complexity of flavour. Winemakers worked out how to re-create this by ageing the wine in hothouses.

---

9 18th-Century Wine Press

A traditional 18th-century wine press **(below)** with the Jesuit symbol of a cross within a triangle is displayed in the courtyard. The Jesuits managed the island's wine trade until the late 18th century. Then English and Scottish merchants took it over.

5 The "Oldest Street"

The street that runs up the eastern side of the wine lodge dates from the 1400s. In the early days of settlement, wine barrels were dragged across the cobbles on a sledge to the harbour.

6 Ageing Room

In the ageing room visitors will find the satin wood vats that contain the wine as it matures. These massive vats are more than 100 years old and can hold more than 9,000 litres (1,980 gallons). The wine is stored here before it is bottled.

8 Wine Shop

This contemporary shop stocks a large selection of wines by producers from the Madeira Wine Company; as well as Madeiran liqueurs, Portuguese table wines and spirits.

10 Goatskins

Wine made all over the island was brought for sale to Funchal. Porters called *borracheiros* sipped from the 40-litre loads of wine that they carried in goatskins.

🔟 ⭐ Museu da Quinta das Cruzes, Funchal

Madeira's early settlers built their homes on the heights above the harbour so that they could see pirate ships approaching. The Quinta das Cruzes is one such estate. Originally built by Captain Zarco, it was later rebuilt as the elegant home of the Lomelino family, and is now a museum full of decorative artwork. A visit can be combined with a stroll to the Convento de Santa Clara nearby.

③ Orchid Garden

A stately old dragon tree *(see p27)* thrusts its fleshy limbs through the roof of the shade house at the rear of the *quinta* garden, where tier upon tier of exquisite tropical orchids are cultivated for use as cut flowers.

① Archaeological Park

The gardens to the south of the *quinta* **(above)** serve as an outdoor museum of archaeological remains. One prominent piece is a fragment of Funchal's pillory, erected in 1486. Until 1835, criminals were chained to the pillory and whipped.

Museu da Quinta das Cruzes floorplan

Entrance

Key
- ▨ Ground Floor
- ▨ First Floor

NEED TO KNOW

MAP N2

Museu da Quinta das Cruzes: Calçada do Pico 1; open 10am–12:30pm & 2–5:30pm Tue–Sun; adm; mqc.gov-madeira.pt

Convento de Santa Clara: Calçada de Santa Clara 15; 291 742 602; open 10am–noon & 3–5pm Mon–Sat; adm

- The museum's garden teahouse has bay views.
- The ticket office will have details of concerts held at the museum.
- It's a steep climb to the museum but taxis and the Route Eco bus also come up here.

② Silver Collection

The rich collection of historic silver reflects the predominant trends in Europe from the 16th to the 19th century. The highlights are a pair of silver and ebony Mexican slave figures and two silver and coral British baby's rattles.

④ Drawing Rooms

Zarco's mansion was a working farm and administrative centre, remodelled by the Lomelino family in the 18th and 19th centuries. Furniture and paintings in the drawing rooms **(left)** were influenced by the British style of the period.

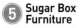

⑤ Sugar Box Furniture

Brazilian sugar put an end to the Madeiran trade. The cupboards in the basement were made from the wooden boxes used to carry the sugar.

⑧ Chapel

The chapel, dating from 1692, contains the tomb of Urbano Lomelino, an early sugar merchant who migrated to the island from Italy in the early 1500s.

CAPTAIN ZARCO: LORD OF THE ISLES

João Gonçalves, who was nicknamed Zarco ("Squinter") after he lost an eye in battle in 1415, planted the Portuguese flag on Porto Santo in 1419, and on Madeira in 1420. In 1425, he returned with people, seeds and tools to live on Madeira. Zarco ruled the island's southwestern half, while fellow captain Tristão Vaz Teixeira ruled the northeast from Machico. Zarco's half proved to have the better harbour, Funchal, which later became the capital. He died in 1467 in Funchal (see p42).

---

⑨ Palanquin

A 19th-century palanquin, used to carry wealthy ladies around Funchal, is displayed on the ground floor. There is also a series of English satirical engravings poking fun at Funchal's well-fed priests and overdressed officials.

⑩ Artwork by Tomás da Anunciação

Picnic **(below)**, by the founder of Portuguese Romanticism, dates from 1865. The family of the second Count of Carvalhal is shown on their Quinta do Palheiro Ferreiro estate (see pp32–3).

⑥ Manueline Windows

The stone window frames **(above)** set in the garden are fine examples of a style inspired by the voyages of discovery made during the reign of King Manuel I of Portugal (1495–1521). They are carved with ships' ropes, leaves, other flora and lions.

⑦ Exhibitions

The museum also hosts a permanent exhibition of decorative arts dating from the 15th to the 19th centuries, which encompasses paintings, sculpture, ceramics, jewellery and furniture, including a display of 19th-century drawings and watercolours of Madeira.

Convento de Santa Clara, Funchal

The cool cloister at the Convento de Santa Clara

1 Cloister

This peaceful spot provided access to chapels and oratories, where the nuns could pass the day in prayer. Admire the cupola of the convent's bell tower from here, decorated with rare 17th-century blue, white and gold ceramic tiles.

2 Abbess's Grave

A gravestone with Gothic script marks the burial place of the convent's first abbess, Isabel de Noronha, and her sister, Constança. As a sign of their humility, these two high-born ladies, whose grandfather was Zarco (see p42), chose to be buried in a corridor where the nuns would walk across their graves each day.

Convento de Santa Clara floorplan

3 Gateway

The arms of the Order of St Francis are carved on the 17th-century stone roundel above the ancient wooden doors of the convent gateway. Ring the bell here to enter.

4 Lower Choir

The lower choir is lined with wooden choir stall chairs dating from 1736, carved with winged cherubs and amusing animal heads. The painted throne was reserved for the use of the bishop and the head of the Franciscan order when they visited.

5 Grille

Through the iron grille in the eastern wall of the lower choir, the congregation could hear the singing of the nuns, and the nuns could hear the priest say mass. The nuns had no other contact with the outside world.

6 Zarco Monument

A coffin-shaped box at the end of the lower choir is a replica of the marble tombstone that stood over Zarco's grave (see p19). It was moved because priests kept tripping over it.

7 Upper Choir

Green Moorish tiles cover the floor of this long room, with its *alfarge* (knotwork) ceiling and gilded altar housing a statue of the Virgin. This choir was the place of daily prayer for the first community of Poor Clare nuns (the sister order to the Franciscans), who came to Santa Clara from Portugal in 1497.

8 Calvary

The large painting of the crucified Christ at the west end of the lower choir served to remind the nuns that their hardships were as nothing compared with his sufferings. Even more poignant is the realistic 17th-century statue of Christ laid in the altar below, as if in his tomb.

9 Monuments

At the back of the church, the stone sarcophagus resting on crouching lions marks the grave of Zarco's son-in-law, Martim Mendes de Vasconcelos (d.1493). Zarco himself, who died in 1467 (see p19), lies buried in front of the high altar, but his tomb slab is hidden beneath a modern wood floor.

10 Church

Santa Clara Church boasts one of Madeira's finest religious interiors, and it can be admired without visiting the rest of the convent. The public part of the church is covered in decorative 17th-century carpet tiles of great intricacy. The magnificent silver tabernacle on the altar dates from 1671.

Tiles on the ceiling of the church

SANTA CLARA CHURCH

Santa Clara Convent is surrounded by high walls, built to shield the nuns from prying eyes and keep them focused on their religious duties without the distractions of the outside world. In the past, the only part of the convent open to the public was the church, with its magnificent silver tabernacle, dating from 1671, and wooden altar, painted to imitate marble and gold. Serene and beautiful, Santa Clara Church is a popular choice for weddings.

TOP 10 DATES IN SANTA CLARA'S HISTORY

1 1476: convent founded
2 1493: church completed
3 1497: nuns move in
4 1566: nuns flee pirates
5 1671: tabernacle unveiled
6 1736: choir stalls carved
7 1797: artists paint church
8 1834: Portugal bans religious orders
9 1890: last nun dies
10 1927: school founded

Secluded and graceful, Santa Clara Convent has preserved some historical treasures.

TOP 10 ⭐ Zona Velha, Funchal

With its choice of lively bars and cafés, celebrated restaurants and compelling visitor attractions, Funchal's Zona Velha (Old Town) is a rejuvenated destination. Centred around ancient, cobbled Rua de Santa Maria, in the early 19th century the neighbourhood was an industrious centre of trade and commerce. Allowed to fall into disrepair and for many years neglected, the maze of narrow streets and their long-abandoned merchants' warehouses once again form a vibrant social hub, complemented by proud local tradition and a fascinating collection of historical and cultural landmarks.

Art Opens Doors ①

Rua de Santa Maria features some amazing examples of street art (**right**). Local artists have painted over many of the neighbourhood's doors, producing art ranging from quirky cartoon murals to abstract designs. There are also examples of sculpture.

② Museu do Brinquedo

Inside the Armazém do Mercado, this toy museum features 20,000 examples of cars, games and dolls donated by José Manuel Borges Pereira and other collectors. The antique items are fascinating. Look out too for rare Star Wars and Action Man collectibles.

④ Jardim do Almirante Reis

This attractive green space fronting Zona Velha is divided into undulating lawns crossed by footpaths. During the summer the garden often hosts arts and crafts fairs and other cultural events.

③ Fortaleza de São Tiago

Squatting above the seafront is this early-17th-century fortress (**below**), instantly recognizable by its chunky, ochre walls. Built to defend the port from pirate attack, the stronghold's castellated battlements, turrets and hidden rooms today make for intriguing exploration (see p67).

⑤ Casa da Luz – Museu de Electricidade

Definitely one to spark the imagination of both adults and kids, the Electricity Museum is set within the city's old power station. Gleaming like new, massive diesel generators stand downstairs while the first floor has a fun, interactive, multimedia "energy sources" exhibition.

7 Madeira Story Centre

The first stop for visitors to Madeira is this inter-active museum **(left)** that describes the island's history and culture, from its volcanic origins to the present day. The impressive exhibition, arranged chronologically, takes a good hour to absorb. Relax afterwards at the rooftop restaurant.

FUNCHAL'S DOOR ART

In 2010 Spanish artist José Maria Zyberchema launched the Art Opens Doors project by using a derelict door in Rua de Santa Maria as a canvas for a mural. A way of brightening up a run-down neighbourhood soon blossomed into permanent street art.

9 Capela do Corpo Santo

The exterior **(below)** of this plain mid-16th-century chapel does not promise much, but once inside the sacred artworks adorning the walls and ceiling are impressive. The portal dates from the 15th century (see p67).

6 Armazém do Mercado

The "Market Warehouse" was created in a former embroidery factory. The pop-up space has artisan boutiques and eateries.

8 Cable Car

The Jardim do Almirante Reis *teléferico* station is the start of the spectacular ride up to Monte (see pp34–5). Kids under six go free.

10 Mercado dos Lavradores

Funchal's busy "Farmers' Market" is an attractive riot of sound and colour, especially on Saturday mornings (see pp24–5).

NEED TO KNOW

Art Opens Doors: **MAP P4–5**; www. arteportasabertas.com

Museu do Brinquedo: **MAP P4**; Rua L Coelho 39; adm; www.armazem domercado.com/museu

Casa da Luz – Museu de Electricidade: **MAP Q4**; Rua Casa da Luz 2; 291 211 480; open 10am–12:30pm 2–6pm Tue–Sat; adm

Armazém do Mercado: **MAP P4**; Rua do Hospital Velho 28; open 10am–8pm daily (to 6pm Sun); www. armazemdomercado.com

Madeira Story Centre: **MAP P5**; Rua D Carlos I 27–29; open 9am–7pm daily; www.madeira storycentre.com

Capela do Corpo Santo: **MAP P4** ■ Rua D Carlos I; open 10am–12:30pm, 2–5pm Mon–Fri

Mercado dos Lavradores: **MAP P4**; Largo dos Lavradores; open 8am–7pm Mon–Thu, 7am–8pm Fri, 7am–2pm Sat

Mercado dos Lavradores, Funchal

Painted blue tiles depicting Leda and the Swan

1 Leda and the Swan
To the right of the entrance porch, a tile picture shows the market as it was at the turn of the 20th century, with canvas awnings and stallholders in traditional costume. The fountain in the picture, topped by a marble statue of *Leda and the Swan*, is now in the town hall courtyard *(see p44)*.

2 Flower Sellers
Today's flower sellers still wear traditional clothes. Their outfits are as colourful and eye-catching as their tropical orchids, bird-of-paradise plants, lilies and flamingo flowers.

3 Butchers and Bars
The butchers' shops, selling fresh, cooked and dried meat and sausages, are in a separate area reached from streets around the market hall. Ringing the perimeter of the hall are hole-in-the-wall bars, where shoppers and market workers snack on little dishes of lupin beans, salty olives or sweet custard pastries.

4 The Market Hall
This Art Deco hall was originally designed in 1937 by Edmundo Tavares (1892–1983). Though it has been built from modern materials, its colours echo the grey and rust-red basalt of traditional Madeiran architecture.

5 Cobbler
You can buy handmade and hard-wearing Madeiran-style ankle boots and stylish leather sandals

A riot of colourful flowers for sale

from Sousa e Sousa. The stall of this cobbler, shaped to resemble a traditional A-frame house *(see p66)*, is located on the right-hand side of the entrance.

6 Tile Pictures
More tile pictures adorn the entrance porch. The work of artist João Rodrigues, made in 1940, depicts stallholders and the coat of arms of Funchal (featuring five sugar cones in a cross).

7 Ground Floor
In the arcades surrounding the central courtyard, you can shop for leather bags and wickerwork, *fado* CDs, Madeira wine and honey cake. Farmers down from the country for the day sell bread, bunches of herbs and seasonal fruits simply from upturned crates.

8 Fruit and Vegetables
Upstairs is the domain of the fruit and vegetable sellers, and it is packed with all manner of colourful and sweet-smelling local produce. As you negotiate the narrow aisles, don't be surprised to be offered a free slice of mango, a passion fruit or a blood-red tomarillo by the stall holders as you pass, in the hope that you will linger and buy.

Tuna fish in the Fish Market

9 Fish Market
If the fruit stalls are a taste of the Garden of Eden, the noisy fish market, in the basement, looks almost like a scene from hell, with its knife-wielding stallholders in blood-stained aprons, hacking into tuna and *espada* fish.

10 Herbalist
On the first floor near the stairs, there is a stall devoted to selling fresh and dried herbs, all carefully labelled. There are bunches of feverfew for headaches, and fennel and eucalyptus sweets to soothe a cold.

THE FRUITS OF MADEIRA

In Funchal's market, even the commonplace can take you by surprise: the tiny honey-scented bananas, no bigger than your finger, are the best you will ever taste. Ignore shiny imported apples and tomatoes in favour of flavoursome varieties that have been grown on the island for centuries. Try locally grown sugar cane, quince, prickly pears, loquats, custard apples, guava, *pitanga* (Brazilian cherries), pawpaw, passion fruit and pomegranate.

Many exotic fruits are sold in Madeira, including these durians and mandarins.

TOP 10 ⭐ Jardim Botânico, Funchal

As well as being a place where avid plant lovers can learn all about the astonishing range of plants that thrive in Madeira's warm and humid climate, this is also a great spot just to relax and enjoy the visual richness of the immaculately maintained flower beds. The gardens occupy the grounds of an estate that once belonged to the Reid family (founders of the world-renowned Reid's Palace) and, with a practised eye for a good location, they chose to build their mansion on a sunny slope blessed with panoramic views.

Carpet Bedding 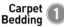 ①

The purple, red, green, yellow, white and gold diamonds, lozenges and circles of this much-photographed part of the estate's garden **(right)** demonstrate the great richness and variety of colour to be found just in the leaves of plants.

② Natural History Museum

The Quinta do Bom Sucesso ("Mansion of Good Fortune"), built in the late 19th century by the Reid family *(see p43)*, was bought by the Madeiran government in 1952. In 1982, the Natural History Museum opened here.

Map of Jardim Botânico, Funchal

③ Coastal Plants

Near to this area, where the palm trees and cycads collection is situated, is a small group of Madeiran indigenous and endemic plant species. These hardy plants manage to thrive on rocky cliffs or along the shoreline.

④ Native Plants

It is useful to be reminded of species that are native to the island. Those growing in beds alongside the museum include giant golden buttercups and Madeiran geranium.

⑤ Parrot Park

The closer you get to the southern part of the garden, the less you will be able to avoid the squawks of the rare and exotic birds **(left)** that are housed in the Parrot Park *(see p59)*.

7 Topiary Garden

This knot garden **(left)** is made of clipped box, and planted with shrubs that can be cut into spirals, pyramids, chess pieces and a variety of animal shapes.

8 Economic Plants

If you cannot tell a mango tree from an avocado, this is the place to learn. The plants grown here are used for food, fibre, oil or dye. Among the examples are several whose names we know but may never have seen, such as coffee, cocoa, sugar cane and cotton.

9 Valley View

The western edge of the garden (furthest from the entrance) has views over the green, canyon-like João Gomes Valley. Though crossed by a road bridge, this is an important wildlife corridor. Huge, ancient parasol pines, with twisted branches and scaly bark, cling to the rocks beside the viewing point *(miradouro)*.

6 Cacti and Succulents

This part of the garden is popular with children for its Wild West look **(below)** and for the many spiders that use the thorns of the cacti as supports for their intricate webs.

DRAGON TREES

If ever a plant looked like its name, the dragon tree *(Dracaena draco)* is it. The fleshlike branches are covered in scaly grey bark that looks and feels rather reptilian, while the leaves are like claws or talons. When cut, the tree "bleeds" a vivid red sap which sets to form a resinous gum known as Dragon's Blood, once highly prized as a dye (it turns cloth purple) and harvested by sailors.

10 Scientific Plants

Staff carry out research using the plants grown in this section to better understand plant taxonomy, reproductive biology and ecology.

NEED TO KNOW

MAP H5 ▪ Quinta do Bom Sucesso, Caminho do Meio ▪ 291 211 200 ▪ www.ifcn.madeira.gov.pt

Open 9am–5:30pm daily

Adm €5.50 (under 6s free)

▪ There is a café set around pretty lotus- and lily-filled ponds.

▪ Some of the best views are to be had from the "Lovers' Cave" at the top of the garden.

▪ Entry to the Jardim Botânico also includes admission to the Jardim dos Loiros, or Parrot Park *(see p59)*. Orchid fans shouldn't miss the Jardim Orquídea, a short, steep walk away.

▪ A cable car gets you to Monte *(see pp34–5)* in around ten minutes.

Plants on Madeira

Native Madeiran geraniums

1 Madeiran Geranium

Also known as cranesbill, the Madeiran geranium (*Geranium maderense*) has become a popular garden plant all over Europe because of its shrubby stature, feathery leaves and large purple-veined magenta flowers.

2 Stink Laurel

The Portuguese took a heavy toll on the huge and ancient laurel trees (*Ocotea foetens*, or *til* in Portuguese) after they arrived on the island in 1420. Felled trunks were shipped to Portugal and Spain for shipbuilding; the ships of the Spanish Armada were largely built from this wood.

3 Giant Buttercups

Madeira's subtropical climate seems to encourage plants to turn into giants. Here, poinsettias grow 4 m (12 ft) tall, and heaths are trees rather than shrubs. This tall shrubby buttercup (*Ranunculus cortusifolia*) is a very handsome plant that looks good anywhere.

4 Madeiran Juniper

Confusingly called *cedro* (cedar) in Portuguese, the dark wood of the Madeiran juniper has a rich patina that can be readily seen in the knotwork ceilings of Funchal Cathedral (*see p13*), Santa Clara Convent (*see p21*) and the church in Calheta (*see p88*).

5 Lily-of-the-valley Tree

You could pass this shrub (*Clethra arborea*, or *folhado* in Portuguese) 9 months out of 12 and not even notice it, but from August to October it is a stunning sight, hung all over with sweet-smelling clusters of bell-like flowers of the purest white.

6 Tree Heath

Related to heather, and with similar pink bell-like flowers, Madeira's tree heaths (*Erica arborea*)

Stink laurel or *til* trees

can grow to a quite prodigious size; a carbonized tree heath trunk in Madeira's Natural History Museum *(see p26)* probably lived for several hundred years. Tree heath branches are used locally for fencing and windbreaks.

⑦ Scented Bay

The essential flavouring ingredient in Madeira's national dish *espetada* (beef kebabs) is the scented bay (*Lauras novocanariensis*, or *loureiro* in Portuguese). It has aromatic evergreen leaves and grows abundantly in the wild.

⑧ Ironwood

Apollonius barbujana (known as *barbusano* in Portuguese) is one of the main constituents of Madeira's native evergreen forest. Its billowing clouds of fresh lime-green coloured

Pride of Madeira bloom

leaves contrast pleasingly with the deep green of the previous years' growth of foliage.

⑨ Pride of Madeira

The plant Pride of Madeira *(Echium candicans)* is almost the symbol of the island. Blooming with an abundance of long-lasting powder-blue flower spikes at exactly the time of year (from December to March) when other flowers are usually shy, it adorns the island's roadsides.

⑩ Madeiran Mahogany

Madeira's museums are full of fine furniture made from *vinhático* *(Persea indica)*, the mahogany-like wood that grows to a great height and girth in the woods. So valuable and costly was sugar in the 15th century that it was shipped to Europe in chests made of this wood.

MADEIRA: WORLD HERITAGE SITE

The primeval woodland that cloaks much of Madeira's mountainous interior is the remnant of the scented laurel forest that covered much of southern Europe until the last Ice Age (which ended around 10,000 years ago). Only on Madeira, the Canaries, the Azores and in tropical west Africa was the climate warm enough for these subtropical trees and shrubs to survive. Known in Portuguese as *laurissilva* (laurel wood), they are a precious link with the past. UNESCO designated a large area of the island's natural forest as a protected World Heritage Site in December 1999.

TOP 10
WILD PLANTS TO SPOT ON A WALK

1 Viper's bugloss
2 Saucer plant (House leek)
3 Navelwort
4 Downy thistle
5 Shrubby sow thistle
6 Ice plant
7 Bilberry
8 Foxglove
9 Dog violet
10 Fleabane

Madeira has a wealth of plants to look out for. These include succulents such as this bright green ornamental aeonium.

Following pages: The central lake in Monte Palace Tropical Garden

TOP 10 ★ Quinta do Palheiro Ferreiro

The unmistakably English character of the Quinta do Palheiro Ferreiro was stamped on the estate by its first owner, the wealthy Count of Carvalhal, whose love of English landscapes led him to include woodland and grassy meadows when the estate was laid out in 1804. Bought by John Blandy, an English wine merchant, in 1885, the *quinta* has remained in the same family ever since, enriched by the plants that Mildred Blandy imported from China, Japan and her native South Africa.

Sunken Garden ①
Water lilies fill the little pool at the centre of this pretty garden **(right)**. Tall cypresses mark its corners; a variety of topiary shapes flank its four sets of stone steps. In the borders, gazanias mix with beetroot-red house leeks.

Chapel ③
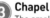
The small, striking Baroque chapel **(left)** has Venetian-style windows and a plasterwork ceiling depicting the baptism of Christ in the River Jordan by John the Baptist.

Camellia Walk ④
Look out for the stone circle called Avista Navios (meaning "Place for Viewing Ships"), where there is a clear view all the way down to the harbour.

Lady's Garden ②

The *Jardim da Senhora* has topiary nesting birds and vintage trees, including a grand old Madeiran *til* tree *(see p28)*, two Canary pines and a weeping *Saphora japonica*, whose spiral limbs and delicate leaves cascade down to form a natural green veil.

NEED TO KNOW

MAP H5 ▪ Caminho da Quinta do Palheiro 32, São Gonçalo ▪ 291 793 044 ▪ www.palheiro gardens.com

Open 9am–5:30pm daily

Adm €10.50 (children 15–17s €4, under 15s free)

▪ The Tea House is at the end of the garden, near an area now run as a golf course *(see p57)*.

▪ A rose garden, near the chapel, has traditional roses and newer varieties brought in from the UK.

▪ Casa Velha is open to hotel guests only.

7 Terrace
Paved with tiny sea-worn pebbles, the terrace **(above)** offers a good view of the house (no admission) that John Blandy built in 1885. He managed successfully to blend the English and the Madeiran architectural styles.

8 Hell Valley
Despite its name, this valley is a delightful tangle of bamboo, tree ferns, native woodland and creepers, with an understorey of beautiful acanthus plants.

9 Stream Garden
The stream you cross to enter the garden is fed by a spring that attracts birds. Lined by azaleas, rhododendrons and scarlet tritonias, it is crossed by pretty bridges.

Map of Quinta do Palheiro Ferreiro

5 Long Borders
Typically English herbaceous border plants, such as delphiniums and day lilies, are mixed with tender and exotic orchids, and angel's trumpets (daturas). Climbing roses and jasmine hang over arches so that you catch their scent as you pass.

10 Long Avenue
Plane trees and giant camellias, many planted 200 years ago, line the avenue. The red, pink and white flowers are at their best from November to April, before white arum lilies and blue agapanthus take over.

6 Casa Velha
Now a luxurious hotel (see p114), the "old house" **(right)** was originally a hunting lodge. Archduchess Leopoldina of Austria stayed here on her way to marry Pedro I of Brazil in 1817.

🔟⭐ Monte

Like the hill stations of colonial India, Monte (literally, "Mount") developed in the late 18th century as a genteel and healthy retreat from the heat, smells, noise and commercial activity of the capital. Funchal's suburbs now spread all the way up to Monte, but there is still a sense of escaping from the city and entering a world set apart. The cool, clear air is filled with birdsong. Few cars intrude onto the cobbled streets, and lush gardens are everywhere – lushest of all, the extraordinary Monte Palace Tropical Garden.

1 Monte Palace Tropical Garden

Lakes, waterfalls and an engaging museum have earned the Monte Palace Tropical Garden **(above)** a name among the most beautiful botanical gardens in the world.

3 Quinta Jardins do Imperador

Just south of Monte is the beautiful mansion where Austrian Emperor Charles I lived in exile. The knot gardens and lake enclose the Malakoff Tower, which houses a café.

4 Monte Cable Car

The cable car's sleek terminus is Monte's only modern building. Along its route up the wild João Gomes Valley, you can see examples of many protected species of native trees and flowers.

Toboggan Run 2

Monte's toboggans **(right)** are steered by smartly dressed *carreiros* (toboggan drivers) in straw boaters on the 2-km (1-mile) trip from Monte to Livramento.

8 Church Steps

On the Feast of the Assumption (15 August), pilgrims climb on their knees up the steps **(left)** to Monte's church to pay homage to the statue of the Virgin. They believe the statue was given by the Virgin when she appeared to a shepherd girl in the 15th century.

5 Parque do Monte

This public park was laid out in 1894 under the railway viaduct draped in *Monstera deliciosa* plants. Cobbled paths lead into a valley of hydrangeas, tree ferns and agapanthus.

9 House of the Pilgrims

This 18th-century building is now used as a cultural centre. It houses an exhibition of paintings devoted to the Emperor Charles I who lived in exile here.

6 Fountain Square

Located in a natural amphitheatre shaded by giant plane trees, Monte's main square is artfully paved with sea-rounded cobbles. The square is named after the marble *fonte* of 1897. In its back wall is a niche housing a statue of the Virgin of Monte – a copy of the one in the church.

10 Quinta do Monte

Converted into a fine hotel *(see p115)*, the 19th-century Quinta do Monte sits in beautiful terraced grounds, open to the public during the day. At the heart of the garden is the Baroque chapel **(above)** of the Quinta do Monte. In the garden gazebo is a small café serving teas.

7 Nossa Senhora do Monte

Our Lady of Monte was inaugurated in 1818, replacing a 15th-century chapel built by Adam Ferreira (the first person to be born on Madeira – along with his twin sister, Eve). The church houses the tomb of Emperor Charles I of Austria.

NEED TO KNOW
MAP H5

Monte Palace Tropical Garden: Caminho do Monte; open 9:30am–6pm daily; www.monte palace.com

Toboggan Run: open 9am–6pm Mon–Sat; fare €25 (€30 for two people, €45 for three)

Quinta Jardins do Imperador: Caminho do Pico; 291 780 460; open 9:30am–5:30pm Mon–Sat; adm (to garden only) €6 (children €3, under 12s free)

Monte Cable Car: www. telefericodofunchal.com

Nossa Senhora do Monte: 291 783 877; open 9am–6pm Mon–Sat, 8am–1pm Sun

■ From Funchal take bus 20 or 21 or the cable car from the Zona Velha or the Jardim Botânico. Return on the Monte toboggan or on foot down the steep Caminho do Monte.

TOP 10 ★ Curral das Freiras

To get a feel for the grandeur of Madeira's mountainous interior visit Curral das Freiras ("Nuns' Refuge"), the hidden valley used by the nuns of Santa Clara Convent whenever pirates attacked the island. There is a little village that now nestles there. From such a beautiful spot, the nuns must have returned to their city convent with a heavy heart. Visiting in 1825, H N Coleridge (the nephew of the English poet) described the Curral as "one of the great sights of the world".

1 Road
Until the road was built in 1969 **(below)**, the only way into the valley was the footpath. The old road is now closed and a modern tunnelled highway connects the valley with the rest of the island.

2 East View
Because of its cauldron-like shape, early explorers thought the Curral das Freiras, with its dramatic cliffs rising sheer to the east, was a collapsed volcano. In fact, the circular form is the result of millions of years of river and rain erosion.

PIRATES AHOY!

Pirates were a serious menace in the early history of Madeira, which is why Funchal has three forts. The worst attack occurred in 1566, when the French pirate Bertrand de Montluc landed at Praia Formosa with 1,000 men and plundered the city's churches and mansions over a 15-day period, massacring all who stood in their way. Montluc gained nothing, dying from a wound he received in the attack.

3 Chestnut Woods
The descent to the village takes you through chestnut woods. The trees bear white, sweetly scented flower stems in August, and produce edible chestnuts in October. Lower down, there is natural *laurissilva* forest (see p29). In June, look out for wild orchids.

4 Miradouro
From the car park in front of the hotel, a short footpath leads up to a *miradouro*, or viewing point **(right)**, located high above the Socorridos Valley. From this spot, the village far down below looks like "Shangri-La" – the utopia of James Hilton's novel *Lost Horizon* (1933).

Igreja Matriz **5**

The church in Curral das Freiras dates from the early 19th century. On the last Sunday in August, a statue of the church's patron saint is carried through streets festooned throughout with colourful flags and paper flowers.

8 Eira do Serrado

Admiring this vista from Eira do Serrado **(left)** is as much a part of a visit to Curral das Freiras as the descent into the village itself. There is a hotel and restaurant, so if you love the romantic view, you can stay for lunch or dinner, or even spend the night *(see p115)*.

9 West View

To the west is a serrated ridge with three prominent peaks: Pico do Cavalho, Pico do Serradhino and, highest of all at 1,654 m (5,427 ft), Pico Grande. The next big valley runs from Ribeira Brava to São Vicente via Encumeada Pass.

6 Footpath

You can walk down to the village along the cobbled footpath that begins in the car park. The path has 52 bends; at the bottom, turn right and walk up to the village. You can return by bus 81.

7 North View

To the north, a road heads up the valley, ending just after it disappears from view. There are plans for a tunnel to take the road to the north coast, risking the Curral's tranquillity.

NEED TO KNOW

MAP G4 ■ www.horarios dofunchal.pt

■ At Sabores do Curral *(see p85)*, delicious local cuisine is served on a terrace with spectacular mountain views.

■ Many tour companies in Funchal offer half-day trips to Curral das Freiras, often including Monte *(see p34)* or Câmara de Lobos *(see p82)*. Most of these trips go only as far as Eira do Serrado, the viewing point above the village.

10 Village

The café owners will urge you to try their chestnut dishes **(above)** including roasted salted chestnuts, rich chestnut soup and sweet chestnut cake. Try the delicious chestnut liqueur *castanha*.

TOP 10 ⭐ Pico do Arieiro

Mountaineering equipment is not needed to get to the top of Madeira's third highest peak, because a road takes you all the way from Funchal to the silence of the summit in less than an hour. The mountain top provides a viewing platform from which to look out over the peaks and ravines of the island's central mountains. From here, you have a chance to study the astonishing rock formations left over from the volcanic upheavals that created the island.

3 Sheep Pens
Livestock has been banned from the Ecological Park to allow Madeiran bilberry and heather to thrive, but sheep and goats graze around the summit and their pens can be seen.

4 West View
The view westward from the summit takes in the full central mountain range, with its succession of knife-edge peaks. The predominant colours are fiery reds, rust browns, blacks and purples of oxidized volcanic rocks, more like the surface of Mars than the Earth.

1 Ice House
This igloo-shaped building **(above)**, 2 km (1 mile) south of the peak, is known as Poço da Neve ("Snow Well"), and was constructed in 1813 by an Italian ice cream maker. Ice from pits like this one provided wealthy hotel guests with so-called "snow water" in the heat of summer.

2 Footpath
A footpath **(below)** links four main peaks and is one of the island's most exciting walks. It should not be attempted unless you are properly equipped for mountain conditions, including sudden storms, tunnels and unprotected drops. A large yellow sign marks the start of the path. Walk the first 100 m (328 ft) or so for fine views back to the summit.

8 Ecological Park

En route from Funchal, after 12 km (7 miles), you pass the entrance to the Ecological Park **(left)**, where primeval forest has been restored. With its viewing points and glades, it is a popular spot for picnics.

5 East View

The view to the east looks down over the green wooded slopes of the island's indigenous forest *(see p29)*. It is possible to see the meadows of Santo da Serra, and the island's long rocky tail.

6 Café

The photographs on the walls of the summit café show the peak at sunset, at sunrise and in snow. They might tempt you to return to enjoy the colours of the sky at dusk or dawn, or to view the night sky away from the glare of city lights.

7 Volcanic Dykes

Another distinctive feature of the view to the west and south is a series of parallel grey outcrops, resembling the Great Wall of China, that follow the contours of the landscape. These are vertical seams of hard volcanic rock that have resisted the erosive forces of rain, frost and wind.

ISLAND ORIGINS

Madeira's long, slow birth began 18 million years ago, as lava burst up through the ocean floor to create layer upon layer of basaltic rock. It took 15 million years for Pico do Arieiro to reach this height. For another 2.25 million years, further eruptions spilled lava sideways from the island's central core, creating the plains of the Paúl da Serra to the west and Santo da Serra to the east.

9 Wildlife

Even on the bare, dry rocks of Madeira's high peaks, plants find a niche wherever a crack provides shelter and moisture. Among the gorse and heather, you can spot grasshoppers and the camouflaged native grayling butterfly.

10 Trig Point

A short scramble up from the café brings you to the actual summit, 1,818 m (5,965 ft) above sea level. It is marked by a concrete post used for measuring altitude and location **(below)**.

The Top 10 of Everything

Dancers performing during the
annual Flower parade on Madeira

Moments in History

1 Island Formation

Twenty million years ago, the Madeiran archipelago began to emerge from the sea (first Porto Santo, then Madeira and the Ilhas Desertas). Pockets of fertile soil were created when storms eroded the softer layers of volcanic ash.

2 Early Visitors

Sailors visited Madeira to gather sap from dragon trees for use in dying clothes. Although mentioned in the *Natural History* of Pliny the Elder (AD 23–79), Madeira was first charted on the Medici Map of 1351, appearing as "Isola de Lolegname" or the "Wooded Isle".

Henry the Navigator in his armour

3 Zarco Arrives

Prince Henry "the Navigator" (1394–1460), third son of King John I of Portugal, realized how valuable Madeira was to sailors exploring the Atlantic Ocean. He sent João Gonçalves Zarco (1387–1467) *(see p19)* to the islands. Zarco landed on Porto Santo, and returned in 1420 to claim Madeira for Portugal.

4 Colonization

Portuguese colonization of Madeira began in 1425, when Zarco returned to govern the southwestern half from Funchal. Tristão Vaz Teixeira controlled the northeastern half, and Bartolomeu Perestrelo governed Porto Santo. Machico was initially the capital, but Funchal had the better harbour and consequently gained city status in 1508.

5 Prosperity

By 1470, the early settlers of Madeira were exporting wheat, dye-stuffs, wine and timber, but sugar produced the biggest profits. Trading with London, Antwerp, Venice and Genoa, the island was Europe's main sugar producer for 150 years, putting the profits into building and art.

6 Wine

Quick profits and wealth became a thing of the past once Caribbean and Brazilian sugar hit European markets in the mid-16th century. *Malvazia* (Malmsey), a rich sweet wine, took over as Madeira's main export. It is the favourite drink of Shakespeare's character Falstaff.

7 The British Arrive

British merchants dominated the wine trade after King Charles II married the Portuguese princess Catherine of Braganza in 1662, and British (and American) taxes on

Catherine of Braganza

Madeira wine were reduced as part of the marriage settlement. So valuable was Madeira to the British, that an armed force was sent in 1801 to stop Napoleon capturing it.

8 Reid's Palace

Once the Napoleonic Wars were over, Madeira became a very popular winter holiday destination for wealthy northern Europeans. Symbolic of the era is Reid's Palace (see p114), founded by William Reid, who arrived a poor sailor in 1836 and made a fortune renting houses to aristocratic visitors.

Soldiers on the streets of Lisbon

9 Autonomy

Madeira escaped the worst effects of the two World Wars, but by 1974, the year of Portugal's Carnation Revolution, it had become Europe's poorest region. In that year, Portugal's dictatorship was toppled in a coup by army officers. Later, celebrating soldiers had carnations stuck in their gun barrels by joyous civilians. In 1976, Madeira became largely autonomous, except for tax, foreign policy and defence.

10 Catastrophe

In 2008, Funchal celebrated its 500th anniversary as the capital of an increasingly prosperous island, but in February 2010, a devastating storm caused widespread floods. Lives were lost, and homes, roads and bridges destroyed. Funchal was particularly affected, although within weeks it was functioning again thanks to the resolve of the islanders.

TOP 10 FAMOUS VISITORS

Statue of Christopher Columbus

1 Robert Machin
This shipwrecked sailor and his lover Anne of Hertford died on Madeira during the 1370s.

2 King Ladislaw III
Having lost the Battle of Varna in 1444, the former king of Poland was one of Madeira's first settlers.

3 Columbus
Arriving as a sugar merchant in 1478–9, Columbus returned in 1498 on his way to the New World for the last time.

4 Captain Kidd
The treasure that pirate Captain Kidd is said to have buried on Ilhas Desertas in the 1690s has never been found.

5 Captain James Cook
The explorer called in at Madeira on his ship, the *Endeavour*, in 1768.

6 Napoleon
The vanquished French emperor was given wine at Funchal on his way to exile on St Helena in 1815.

7 Emperor Charles I
The last Austro-Hungarian emperor, Charles I, died in exile on Madeira in 1922 (see p35).

8 George Bernard Shaw
Visiting in 1927, the Irish playwright praised his local dancing instructor as "the only man who ever taught me anything".

9 Winston Churchill
Churchill wrote *The Hinge of Fate* (volume 4 of his memoirs) while staying at Reid's Hotel in 1949.

10 Margaret Thatcher
The future British prime minister, Margaret Thatcher, spent her honeymoon at the Savoy Hotel, Funchal, in 1951.

Historic Buildings

1 Capela do Corpo Santo, Funchal

This 16th-century chapel situated in the Zona Velha (Old Town) was built and run by the Guild of São Pedro Gonçalves, a self-help charity that raised funds for fishermen and their families (see pp22–3).

2 Capela de Santa Catarina, Funchal

MAP Q2 ■ Jardim de Santa Catarina

Founded in 1425 by Constança de Almeida, Zarco's wife, this chapel was the first to be built in Funchal.

Interior of the Fishermen's Chapel

3 Fishermen's Chapel, Câmara de Lobos

MAP F6 ■ Câmara de Lobos

This simple, moving chapel on the harbour is where fishermen come to pray before and after going to sea. Wall paintings depict the story of how St Anthony of Padua (who was born in Lisbon) survived a shipwreck, and was so eloquent that even the fishes of the sea came to hear him preach.

Câmera Municipal town square

4 Tower House, Funchal

MAP P3 ■ Rua do Bispo

Opposite the Museum of Sacred Art (see pp14–15) is a stately building with a *torre-mirante* (viewing tower). Typical of the grander of Funchal's townhouses, these towers were built for the owners to see incoming ships. Note that the door handles are made from large iron keys.

5 House of the Consuls, Funchal

MAP P3 ■ Rua de Conceição ■ Closed to the public

Few traditional Madeiran houses are more ornate than this 18th-century house built for foreign diplomats.

6 Igreja Inglesa, Funchal

MAP P2 ■ Rua do Quebra Costas

The English Church (1822) is a domed Neo-Classical building set in a delightful garden. Its construction was funded by public appeal; contributions came from Nelson, George II and the Duke of Wellington.

7 Câmara Municipal, Funchal

MAP P3 ■ Praça do Município ■ Ask the porter for permission to view the courtyard

Madeira's early 19th-century town hall originally belonged to the Count of Carvalhal (see p32). Look in the inner courtyard to see graceful balconies and a sensuous statue of *Leda and the Swan* (1880), brought here when the market was built in 1937 (see p24).

Funchal's Banco de Portugal

⑧ Banco de Portugal, Funchal

MAP P3 ■ Avenida Zarco

The Bank of Portugal building (1940) maintains continuity with traditional architecture, with its globe-topped corner turret, Grecian marble statues, and fruit-filled baskets symbolizing wealth and plenty. Just across the road is Francisco Franco's *Zarco Monument* (1927), showing Funchal's founder looking out to sea.

⑨ Alfândega, Funchal

MAP P3 ■ Rua da Alfândega ■ 291 210 500 ■ By appointment

Designed in 1508 by Pêro Anes (who also designed the cathedral), the Customs House was built to collect the taxes levied by the Portuguese Crown on Madeira's timber, corn and sugar exports. Now home to the island's Regional Assembly, it has three splendid upper-floor rooms.

⑩ Administrative Offices, University of Madeira, Funchal

MAP P3 ■ Rua dos Ferreiros

The 17th-century buildings of what used to be the old Jesuit college have now been restored to provide new administrative offices for the University of Madeira. From the inner courtyard, there are good views of the Igreja do Colégio tower *(see p46)*.

TOP 10 FLAMBOYANT BUILDINGS IN FUNCHAL

1 The Ritz Restaurant
The former Chamber of Commerce on Avenida Arriaga, clad in tile pictures of Madeiran transport, now serves as an upscale restaurant.

2 New Chamber of Commerce
Today's Chamber of Commerce is located in a 15th-century building off Rua dos Aranhas.

3 Pátio
The inner courtyard of the 1860s Pátio (Rua da Carreira 43) features a sweeping double staircase leading to the Vicentes Museum.

4 Rua da Carreira
On this street of flamboyant iron balconies, look out especially for those at numbers 77–91 and 155.

5 Rua da Mouraria
Funchal's antiques quarter has many aristocratic townhouses, including the Museu Municipal *(see p49)*.

6 Garden Gazebo
Take tea, admire the views and watch the world go by at a *casinha de prazer* ("pleasure house") like the one in the Freitas Museum *(see p48)*.

7 Quintas
Ornate mansions like the Quinta Palmeira and its gardens *(see p50)* line the terraces above Funchal.

9 Casino
The 1970s casino on Avenida do Infante looks wonderful lit up at night.

9 Apartamentos Navio Azul
Reminiscent of an ocean liner, this curvy 1970s block stands next to the Estrada Monumental.

10 Madeira Cable Car Station
This public building is a futuristic cube of steel and glass on Rua Dom Carlos.

The Ritz Restaurant, Funchal

⓾ Churches

Glorious interior of Igreja do Colégio, Funchal, filled with colourful frescoes

① Igreja do Colégio, Funchal

MAP P3 ■ Praça do Município

The Jesuits, a large brotherhood of missionary priests, owned huge wine estates on Madeira and spent some of their wealth on this lovely church, which is covered from floor to ceiling in frescoes, gilded carvings and rare ceramic tiles. The school the Jesuits built alongside the church is now the University of Madeira.

② Igreja do São Pedro, Funchal

MAP N2 ■ Rua do São Pedro

The main church until the cathedral was built, St Peter's has a wealth of gilded woodwork, some dating from the 17th century. The corn and grapes being gathered by angels in the right-hand chapel are symbolic of the bread and wine of Christ's Last Supper. A simple slab covers the grave of João de Mourarolim (died 1661), who paid for the decoration.

③ São Salvador, Santa Cruz

MAP K5

This Gothic parish church was completed in 1512, when the tomb of the merchant Micer João, supported by crouching lions, was installed on the north side. Next to it is the chapel of the Morais family (1522). The altar has 16th-century paintings depicting the life of Christ by Gregório Lopes, and the sacristy, entered through a Manueline portal, contains a 16th-century carved and painted tableau of the *Last Supper*.

④ Funchal Cathedral (Sé)

The 15th-century cathedral of Funchal is a unique blend of Portuguese, Spanish, Italian and Flemish styles. It set the pattern for the island's other churches with its beautiful *talha dourada* ("gilded woodwork"), as demonstrated in the Holy Sacrament chapel, located to the right of the high altar *(see pp12–13)*.

Statue, Funchal Cathedral

5 Igreja da Nossa Senhora da Conceição, Machico
MAP K4
Probably designed by Pêro Anes, who designed Funchal Cathedral, this church dates from 1499 and is noted for its south door – the white marble pillars come from Seville and were a gift from King Manuel I (1495–1521). So, too, was the statue of the Virgin kept in its tabernacle at the peak of the elaborately gilded high altar.

6 Capela dos Milagres, Machico
MAP K4
The Chapel of the Miracles takes its name from the 15th-century Flemish crucifix on the high altar. It was miraculously found floating at sea, years after the old chapel was washed away by a flood in 1803. The original chapel is said to have been built over the grave of Anne of Hertford and Robert Machin, legendary lovers shipwrecked here in the 14th century.

7 Santa Clara, Funchal
Founded in 1476 by João Gonçalves de Câmara, son of Zarco (see p19), this convent has changed very little since it was first built (see pp20–21).

8 Senhora da Luz, Ponta do Sol
MAP D5
Founded in 1486 by Rodrigo Anes, one of the first men to be granted land on Madeira by the Portuguese king, this attractive church has an original knotwork ceiling, a 16th-century Flemish altarpiece, as well as a unique ceramic font, glazed with green copper oxide to resemble bronze.

9 São Bento, Ribeira Brava
MAP D5
A lion and a basilisk (whose stare was said to turn humans to stone) are among the carvings on the capitals, font and pulpit of this Gothic parish church. Don't miss the magnificent 16th-century Flemish *Nativity* panels showing São Bento and São Bernardo and the statue of the Virgin.

Church of São Bento, Ribeira Brava

10 Capela do Loreto, Loreto
MAP C4
An unspoiled, historic 16th-century church, this boasts a knotwork ceiling and Gothic doorways of imported white marble. The altar was remodelled in the 18th century.

🔟 Museums

Museum Henrique e Francisco Franco

1 Museum Henrique e Francisco Franco, Funchal

MAP N4 ▪ Rua João de Deus 13 ▪ 291 230 633 ▪ 9:30am–6:30pm Mon–Fri ▪ Adm

The Franco brothers, painter Henrique (1883–1961) and sculptor Francisco (1855–1955), left Madeira to find fame in Lisbon and Paris. Their artistic achievements are celebrated in this museum.

Casa Museu Frederico de Freitas

2 Museu da Quinta das Cruzes, Funchal

This is the house where Madeira's first ruler lived when Madeira was the newest addition to Portugal's overseas colonies at the start of the great Age of Discovery in the 15th century. Paintings and sketches of the island's major landmarks hang on the walls of the *quinta*'s richly decorated rooms *(see pp18–19)*.

3 Museu de Arte Sacra, Funchal

Funchal's Religious Art Museum is known for its colourful 16th-century Flemish paintings, but also contains many remarkable polychrome wooden statues *(see pp14–15)*.

4 Blandy's Wine Lodge, Funchal

A guided visit to this vintage Madeira wine lodge is a pleasant sensory experience *(see pp16–17)*.

5 Casa Museu Frederico de Freitas, Funchal

MAP P2 ▪ Calçada de Santa Clara 7 ▪ 291 202 570 ▪ 10am–5:30pm Tue–Sat ▪ Adm

Packed with antiques and religious paintings, this museum also has an amusing collection of teapots from all over the world. A wing is devoted to ceramic tiles, with early examples from long-gone Madeiran churches.

6 Museu a Cidade do Açúcar, Funchal

MAP P3 ▪ Praça Colombo 5 ▪ 291 236 910 ▪ 9:30am–5:30pm Mon–Fri ▪ Adm

Funchal's history is chronicled in fascinating detail by exploring its once-thriving sugar cane industry.

7 Museu Municipal e Aquário, Funchal

MAP P2 ▪ Rua da Mouraria 31 ▪ 291 229 761 ▪ 10am–6pm Tue–Sun ▪ Adm

This museum offers an aquarium downstairs, and stuffed fish, birds and other Madeiran wildlife upstairs.

8 Centro das Artes Casa das Mudas, Calheta

MAP B4 ▪ Estrada Simão Gonçalves da Câmara 37 ▪ 291 820 900 ▪ 10am–1pm & 2–6pm Tue–Sun ▪ Adm

The works of artists such as Picasso and Francis Bacon have been exhibited at this gallery.

Blue whale model at Museu da Baleia

9 Museu da Baleia, Caniçal

MAP L4 ▪ Rua da Pedra d'Eira ▪ 291 961 858 ▪ Open 11am–6pm Tue–Sun ▪ Adm ▪ www.museudabaleia.org

Madeira's Whale Museum welcomes visitors to a world of dolphins and whales. Interactive and 3D displays depict the evolution of these fascinating creatures. Exhibits include a whaling boat.

10 Madeira Story Centre, Funchal

This is an excellent interactive museum covering all aspects of the island's history (see p23). There's also a rooftop restaurant and a shop selling crafts.

TOP 10 MUSEUM EXHIBITS

Tiles at Blandy's Wine Lodge

1 Processional Cross
Superb Renaissance silverwork, with the Evangelists and biblical scenes in relief (Museu de Arte Sacra) (see p14).

2 Max Römer Murals
Scenes depicting the traditional grape harvest celebrate the vigour of youth and the golden light of autumn at Blandy's Wine Lodge (see p16).

3 Indian Miniature
In this exquisite small painting, the Virgin is depicted as a Mogul princess (Room 1, Quinta das Cruzes) (see p18).

4 Wood Sculpture
Rare tribal sculpture from Zimbabwe dating from the 1950s and 1960s (Monte Palace Museum) (see p35).

5 City Coat of Arms
Unusual example from 1584 depicting elements of sugar cane iconography (Museu a Cidade do Açúcar).

6 Moray Eels
Sharp-fanged denizens of the deep (Museu Municipal e Aquário).

7 Winter Garden
Fern-filled, Art Nouveau glass conservatory at the Casa Museu Frederico de Freitas.

8 Boy with Cockerel
This portrait of a Madeiran peasant boy is one of Henrique Franco's best (Museu Henrique e Francisco Franco).

9 Portraits of Columbus
Paintings and drawings of Christopher Columbus (1451–1506) line the walls of the legendary explorer's house (Casa Museu Cristóvão Colombo) (see p102).

10 Scrimshaws
Whalebones carved and etched in the days before hunting whales was illegal (Museu da Baleia).

🔟 Gardens

1 Monte Palace Tropical Garden, Monte

This intriguing botanical garden has caves, fountains, lakes, fish ponds, Japanese temples, sculptures, novel tile pictures as well as a museum *(see p34)*.

Statue in Monte Palace Tropical Garden

2 Santa Catarina Park, Funchal

MAP Q2 ▪ Avenida do Infante ▪ Free

Located on the way from downtown Funchal to the Hotel Zone, this terraced park has fantastic views over the harbour. Look out for the statues of Henry the Navigator at the lower end, Christopher Columbus by the Capela de Santa Catarina *(see p44)* and the 1919 *Semeador* or the "Sower" by Francisco Franco *(see p48)*, symbolically throwing handfuls of seed across the grass.

3 Quinta das Cruzes, Funchal

The flower-filled grounds of this "archaeological park" *(see p18)* boasts grave slabs, a private chapel, a wonderful orchid garden and a *casinha de prazer* ("pleasure house"), perched on the walls to take advantage of the views *(see pp18–19)*.

Display of flowers, Jardim Botânico

4 Ribeiro Frio Forest Park

MAP H4 ▪ São Roque do Faial ▪ 291 575 434

The park comprises a wide area of the UNESCO-listed *laurissilva* forest. Hikers will find several fantastic mountain walks here, such as the Levada do Furado *(see p55)*. For others, the village has a trout farm to visit and a rustic restaurant to enjoy *(see p83)*.

5 Quinta Palmeira, Funchal

MAP G6 ▪ Rua da Levada de Santa Luzia 31A ▪ 291 221 091 ▪ 10am–4pm Tue–Wed (advance booking only) ▪ Adm

Despite being blighted by its proximity to one of Funchal's fast highways, this former home of the Gordon wine family hovers between garden and wilderness, with manicured rose gardens, tiled fountains, grottoes and some jungle-like areas. Don't miss the 15th-century Columbus Window, rescued from the home of João Esmeraldo.

6 Jardim Botânico, Funchal

These extraordinary gardens are a showcase for Madeira's varied plant life *(see pp26–9)*.

⑦ Jardins Quinta da Boa Vista

Visit this wonderfully appealing subtropical garden complex between December and May to witness the orchid collection in all its exquisite finery. The rest of the estate is dedicated to re-creating the habitats of endangered plant species *(see p64)*.

⑧ Quinta Vigia, Funchal
MAP Q1 ▪ Avenida do Infante

The well-kept gardens of Madeira's president are open on weekdays, so long as there are no official functions.

Fountain in Quinta Vigia, Funchal

⑨ Quinta do Palheiro Ferreiro

Situated in an enviable location above Funchal, unusual and imaginative subtropical plants are displayed here in a style that is recognizably English *(see pp32–3)*.

⑩ Jardim de São Francisco, Funchal
MAP P2 ▪ Avenida Arriaga ▪ Free

St Francis, the patron saint of the environment, would firmly approve of this richly planted garden, built in the city centre on the site of Funchal's long-gone Franciscan friary. It is only the size of a city block, but so full of scented and flowering plants, shaded by some truly enormous trees, that you could be in the middle of the jungle.

TOP 10 MADEIRAN PLANTS AND FLOWERS

Beautiful king protea plants

1 King Protea
These South African plants, similar to giant artichokes, are in demand for flower displays.

2 Slipper Orchid
Mainly flowering in the winter months, slipper orchids need jungle-like shade.

3 Mexican Poinsettia
These festive plants bloom right on cue for Christmas; note that the showy, scarlet part is actually the bract, not the flower.

4 Aloe
Fleshy leaves edged with spines produce flower spikes up to 1 m (3 ft) high. The sap is harvested, and used in making aloe vera skin products.

5 Agapanthus
The blue-and-white globe-shaped blossoms of the Lily of the Nile line Madeira's roadside banks in summer.

6 Strelitzia
Is it a bird or is it a plant? These long-lived flowers look like exotic birds of paradise.

7 Angel's Trumpet
White, yellow or amber, the datura's long trumpets smell and look lovely.

8 Arum Lily
Pure white and sweetly scented, these flowers symbolize the Virgin Mary and virginity.

9 Flame of the Forest
Crowned by orange-red coxcombs, these trees are descended from the seeds brought to Madeira by Captain Cook in 1772.

10 Jacaranda
Funchal's Avenida Arriaga turns into a river of blue when these striking Brazilian trees flower in spring.

Beaches

Glorious, wide stretch of golden sand at Porto Santo

1 Porto Santo
MAP L2

Travel 40 km (25 miles) northeast of Madeira *(see p109)* to enjoy the vast stretch of unspoilt golden sand of Porto Santo *(see p102)*. The Fontinha section offers ramps, toilets and amphibian-use wheelchairs.

2 Calheta
MAP B4

With golden sand specially imported from Morocco, this artificial beach is protected by two breakwaters and is popular, getting crowded during the summer. There are watersports facilities here – this is a great launch pad for canoeists and windsurfers.

3 Prainha
MAP L4

A pretty, sheltered bay with a café at its eastern end, pocket-sized Prainha ("Little Beach") has one of Madeira's naturally sandy beaches.

Prainha's sand beach

4 São Tiago
MAP Q6

A small pebble beach sited under the shadow of Fortaleza de São Tiago *(see p22)*, this is a popular summer destination for locals. A promenade set alongside the fortress walls has extra sunbathing spots. Natural rock formations add to the allure of the beach with its warm shallow water. There are freshwater showers.

5 Praia Formosa
MAP G6

Steep-sided Madeira does not have many beaches – cliffs and rocky shores are the norm – but this, the "Beautiful Beach", is a stretch of grey, sea-smoothed pebbles situated between Funchal and Câmara de Lobos. There are changing facilities, a lifeguard post and also a children's playground at the location.

6 Machico
MAP K4

Positioned near the original basalt pebble beach is the town's artificial alternative, made with sand imported from the Western Sahara in North Africa. The luxuriously soft beach, known as Banda d'Além, is 125 m (410 ft) in length and 70 m (230 ft) wide. It is popular with locals as well as tourists, especially at weekends.

7 Ponta do Sol
MAP D5

The beach at Ponta do Sol ("Sun Point") is the perfect place to watch the setting sun. Dramatic clouds float like islands in a sky coloured pink and purple.

8 Garajau and Caniço
MAP J6

A path from the statue of Christ the Redeemer at Garajau winds down to a beach popular for snorkelling and diving. It marks the start of a marine reserve with underwater caves leading to Caniço de Baixo (see p57).

9 Praia dos Reis Magos
MAP J6

Continuing eastwards from Caniço de Baixo, a seafront promenade leads to Praia dos Reis Magos, a rocky beach with a scattering of fishermen's huts as well as a couple of simple cafés selling freshly grilled fish.This is an idyllic spot for romantics who prefer to be away from the crowds.

Beach and rock pools near São Jorge

10 São Jorge
MAP H2

About 2 km (1 mile) east of São Jorge, a sign to praia ("beach") leads to the estuary of the São Jorge river, where you can swim in a natural pool or in the sea (access via the small pebbled beach). There's a simple beach café.

TOP 10 NATURAL SWIMMING POOLS AND BATHING COMPLEXES

Natural rock pools, Porto Moniz

1 Ponta Delgada
- MAP F2 - Adm
Two seawater pools, with shower facilities and other amenities.

2 Reid's
- MAP G6 - Adm
Modern lido with café on the side of the harbour, with access to the sea.

3 Porto Moniz
- MAP C1 - Adm
Natural rock pools famous across the island. Lockers plus summer snack bar.

4 Porta Gorda
- MAP G6 - Adm
Adventure pools great for kids, while adults can sunbathe looking out to sea.

5 Porto da Cruz
- MAP J3 - Adm
Sun loungers and umbrellas around two swimming pools on the rocky coastline.

6 Seixal
- MAP D2
Close to Laje Beach, natural pools in a lovely landscape with very clear water.

7 Ribeira Brava
- MAP D5
A pebble and black sand beach with a pool facility, which has changing rooms, toilets and restaurant.

8 Barreirinha
- MAP Q5 - Adm
Pool and sunbathing area at São Tiago Beach, with lockers, toilets and a bar.

9 Calhau de São Jorge
- MAP H2 - Adm
Located near Santana, this pool complex provides a safe swimming haven next to an often-rough sea.

10 Doca do Cavacas
- MAP G6 - Adm
Natural volcanic pools enclosed by sculpted rock peer out over open sea. Access via Funchal's Lido promenade.

TOP 10 Levada Walks and Hiking Trails

Cliffs of Ponta de São Lourenço

1 Ponta de São Lourenço
MAP M4

The easternmost peninsula on the island, Ponta de São Lourenço (see p94) makes for a bracing there-and-back coastal amble over undulating, often vertiginous landscape. Starting at the Baía d'Abra car park, the trail follows the peninsula's pointed finger and gives impressive Atlantic views. There is little shade, and strong gusts are commonplace.

2 Pico do Arieiro–Pico Ruivo
MAP G4

This challenging mountain hike connects Madeira's third-highest peak, Pico do Arieiro (see pp38-39) with the highest, Pico Ruivo. You'll also scale the second-highest, Pico das Torres. Take warm clothing, plenty of water and a torch for the tunnels. A guide is recommended or climb as part of an organized hike.

Along the Pico do Arieiro

3 Levada do Norte
MAP G6

A lengthy but comfortable walk along the popular Levada do Norte that conveniently begins at a bus stop in Estreito de Câmara de Lobos. There is the option of a detour to Cabo Girão (see p81). Otherwise the trail travels west through a cultivated landscape of vineyards and sugar cane.

4 Prazeres–Paúl do Mar
MAP B3

A bracing coastal jaunt that begins in Prazeres (see p90), the path corkscrews down to the sea and skirts a lovely waterfall, with panoramic views across Madeira's southwest region.

5 Santana–São Jorge–Vigia
MAP H2

From Santana there is an occasionally precipitous route that snakes above a restless sea. The track passes Quinta do Furão (see p85) and edges up a narrow path before descending to São Jorge. From here it's a scenic stroll to the lighthouse crowning Vigia.

6 Levada da Serra
MAP D3

Set along the eastern flanks of the Paúl da Serra (see p89), this walk affords marvellous views of the undulating plateau towards the high peaks of Bica da Cana. Part of the trail passes below cascading waterfalls – a majestic and awe-inspiring sight. Note that the route can be very wet, even in summer.

7 Boca da Corrida–Encumeada
MAP G4

Called Caminho Real da Encumeda ("Royal Road"), this trail crosses part of Madeira's central massif and runs along the foot of some of the island's highest peaks. Boca da Corrida marks the start, below which is Curral das Freiras *(see pp36–7)*.

8 Rabaçal–Levada do Risco–Levada das 25 Fontes
MAP C3

A tumbling waterfall near Rabaçal *(see p87)* marks the start of these *levada* walks. Bubbling springs, crystal clear pools and lagoons also appeal. Take care at the Ribeira Grande.

Hiking to Caldeirão Verde

9 Queimadas–Levada do Caldeirão Verde–Santana
MAP H3

The trail that winds the walkways of this scenic *levada* leads to Verdant Queimadas but it also takes in spectacular ravines, cascading waterfalls and four moss-textured tunnels – don't forget to bring a torch!

10 Levada do Furado
MAP H4

One of the oldest *levadas* starts at Ribeiro Frio *(see p83)*, 860 m (2,820 ft) above sea level. A watercourse snakes through paths in the rock, then descends to the village of Portela.

TOP 10 COAST AND MOUNTAIN VIEWPOINTS

1 Pico do Arieiro
MAP G4
The summit of the third-highest peak on the island can be reached by road.

2 Cabo Girão
MAP E5
A glass floor adds to the giddy view over one of Europe's tallest sea cliffs.

3 Morro do Furado
MAP M4
On a clear day you can see Porto Santo Island from this lofty standpoint at the end of Ponta de São Lourenço.

4 Boca da Corrida
MAP F4
Magnificent mountain vistas including Curral das Freiras can be admired from this popular viewpoint.

5 Portela
MAP J4
Panoramas from Miradouro da Portela embrace Penha de Águia *(see p84)*.

6 Balcões
MAP H4
Hikers enjoy views of the Ribeira da Metade Valley, near Ribeiro Frio *(see p83)*.

7 Cabanas
MAP G2
Between São Jorge *(see p84)* and Arco de São Jorge, the view is laced with salt.

8 Bica da Cana
MAP E3
Marked with a cairn, the outlook here takes in high peaks and drifting cloud.

9 Rabaçal
MAP C3
Head for Pico da Urze, in Paúl da Serra, for valley views and *laurissilva* forest.

10 Eira do Serrado
MAP F4
A footpath from the Eira do Serrado hotel *(see p115)* offers a mountain panorama.

Eira do Serrado viewpoint

Outdoor Activities

① Bird-Watching
Madeira Wind Birds: MAP H5; 917 777 441; www.madeirawindbirds. com (for expeditions)

The Madeira archipelago offers excellent opportunities for birders. The islands are home to 42 breeding species, three of which are endemic to Madeira: these are the Zino's petrel, the Trocaz pigeon and the Madeira firecrest. Seabirds are prevalent, while Berthelot's pipit is always a prized sighting.

② Windsurfing
Mar Dourado: MAP L2; 963 970 789

For the most part fanned by gentle sea breezes, the shallow, remarkably clear water lapping at Porto Santo beach (see p102) is perfectly suited to windsurfing. Mar Dourado, located on the expansive sands below the Torre Praia Hotel, offers expert windsurfing. Board and equipment hire is also available. The company organizes a range of watersports activities (see p104).

Windsurfing in Funchal harbour

Mountain biking on a rocky slope

③ Mountain Biking
Terras de Aventura: MAP G6; 291 708 990; www.terrasdeaventura. net

The island's rugged terrain presents challenging tracks as well as gravity-defying inclines. Following *levada* (see pp54–5) footpaths is an easier option. Rent or join an organized excursion.

④ Horse Riding
Quinta do Riacho: MAP J4; 967 010 015; www.quintadoriacho. com ■ Escapada dos Caveleiros: MAP F5; 966 312 151; www.escapadados cavaleiros.com

Several companies in Madeira offer horse riding activities, lessons and guided tours along mountain tracks and forest byways. There are similar options on Porto Santo (see p104).

⑤ Adventure Sports
Terras de Aventura: MAP G6; 291 708 990; www.terrasdeaventura. com ■ Lokoloko: MAP J6; 969 570 780; www.lokolokomadeira.com

Madeira's countryside offers plenty of adventure sports, from trekking and rock climbing to hang gliding and orienteering. Companies such as Terras de Aventura and Lokoloko provide organized excursions.

⑥ Walking
With more than 1,600 km (994 miles) of footpaths, it's no wonder that thousands of people visit to walk in the island's mountains and forests.

7 Boat Trips

Madeira Boat Trips: MAP Q3; Funchal Marina; 969 351 568/ 918 375 661 ▪ Bonita da Madeira: MAP Q3; Funchal Marina; 291 762 218

Booths located around Funchal's marina have details of all the cruising options available, from day-long trips to the Ilhas Desertas *(see p95)* to shorter sunset cruises.

8 Deep-Sea Fishing

Turipesca: MAP Q3; Funchal Marina; 291 231 063 ▪ Balancal: MAP Q3; Funchal Marina; 291 790 350 ▪ Nautisantos: MAP Q3; Funchal Marina; 291 231 312

Fishing trips can be booked at the marina. A tag-and-release policy means fish are put back into the wild.

9 Golf

Clube de Golfe de Santo da Serra: MAP K4; 291 550 100 ▪ Palheiro Golf: MAP J5; Sítio do Balancal, São Gonçalo; 291 790 120

Two of Europe's most scenic courses are located in the east of the island at Santo da Serra and Palheiro Ferreira. Transport can be arranged from Funchal, and equipment hired.

Scuba diver watching a school of fish

10 Diving

Manta Diving Center: MAP J6; Hotel Galomar, Caniço de Baixo; 291 935 588 ▪ Madeira Divepoint: MAP H6; Pestana Carlton Madeira Hotel, Largo Antonio Nobre, Funchal; 291 239 579

Clean Atlantic waters with clear visibility and an array of beautiful fish and reefs have made Madeira a popular spot for divers of all ages and all abilities.

TOP 10 MADEIRAN WILDLIFE

Red-breasted robin

1 Wall Lizards
You will see them on every sunny rock or pavement. They eat fruit and flies.

2 Wagtails
This yellow-breasted bird is never very far from water, hence its Madeiran nickname: "the washerwoman".

3 Swifts
Watch them wheeling and feeding at dusk along Funchal's seafront.

4 Kestrels
These chestnut-backed birds nest on the cliffs of the hotel district, and hover on the wind in search of prey.

5 Buzzards
These birds are often seen riding the warm air above the valleys of Funchal and Curral das Freiras.

6 Robins
The robins you will see on Madeira have the same cheery red breasts as their mainland cousins, and just as sweet a song.

7 Sally Lightfoot Crabs
These dark brown crabs are often seen grazing tidal rocks for algae. They will disappear fast if threatened – hence their "lightfoot" name.

8 Perez's Frogs
Introduced to Madeira by the Count of Carvalhal, this noisy frog with a bright yellow backbone stripe has spread to every pond in the island.

9 Monarch butterflies
These large orange-black-and-white gliding butterflies are seen in all Madeiran gardens.

10 Limpets
Limpets are a traditional food on Madeira, but harvesting is controlled to prevent over-exploitation.

🔟 Children's Attractions

① Grutas de São Vicente
MAP E2 ■ São Vicente, Sítio do Pé do Passo ■ 291 842 404 ■ Open 10am–6pm daily ■ Adm ■ www.grutasecentrodovulcanismo.com

These caves were created by molten rock. A cave tour, simulated eruptions and a short film teaches both children and adults about the volcanic origins of Madeira.

Volcanic caves at São Vicente

② Madeira Theme Park
MAP H2 ■ Estrada Regional 101, Fonte da Pedra, Santana ■ 291 570 410 ■ Open 10am–7pm daily (to 6pm Oct–Mar) ■ Closed mid-Jan–mid-Jun: Mon; Sep–mid-Dec ■ Adm ■ www.parquetematicodamadeira.pt

Set around a boating lake, the park boasts a number of pavilions devoted to the island's heritage and traditions. There's a maze to get lost in and a radical sports zone to check out. Children also have their own playground.

③ Santa Catarina Park
Offering a very attractive view out over Funchal Bay, these beautiful public gardens (see p50) also feature a children's playground and a palm-fringed lake where youngsters will enjoy feeding the resident swans and ducks while adults take a pause.

④ Dolphin-Watching
MAP Q3 ■ Tickets from Marina do Funchal ■ 291 231 312 ■ Adm

Few encounters with nature are as exciting as those with dolphins or whales in their natural habitat, but this trip will appeal to older children, because a patient wait does not always mean the animals will make an appearance.

⑤ Aquaparque
MAP K5 ■ Ribeira da Boavista, Santa Cruz ■ 291 524 412 ■ Open Jun–Nov: 10am–6pm daily (till 7pm Aug) ■ Adm

This fabulous landscaped water park features twisting slides, rapids and waterfalls. The Infant Zone's shallow pool and "lazy river" is ideal for toddlers.

⑥ Santa Maria de Colombo
MAP Q3 ■ Tickets from Marina do Funchal ■ 291 220 327 ■ Trips 10:30am–1:30pm & 3–6pm daily ■ Adm ■ www.madeirapirateboat.com

There are many boat trips to choose from (see p57), but children will particularly enjoy a trip on a replica of the Santa Maria, the ship that took Christopher Columbus across the Atlantic on his first voyage from Europe to the Americas.

Cruising on the Santa Maria

Statue of footballer Cristiano Ronaldo

7 Museu CR7

MAP Q2 ■ Av. Sá Carneiro–Praça do Mar 27, Funchal ■ 291 639 880 ■ Open 10am–6pm daily ■ Adm ■ www.museucr7.com

A must for all football fans, especially any enamoured by Cristiano Renaldo and his number 7 shirt. The trophies and medals awarded the Madeira-born, Portuguese international are showcased in suitably dazzling fashion.

8 Monte Cable Car

The Monte *teléferico* or cable car *(see p34)* flies spectacularly high over the João Gomes Valley, with children under six travelling for free. Once in Monte, you can explore the Palace Tropical Garden *(see p34)*.

9 Parrot Park

Children may either enjoy the antics of parrots and parakeets, or, if they are older, engage in a discussion about the ethics of keeping wild creatures in cages for amusement. While you're here, you can explore the Botanical Garden *(see pp26–7)*.

10 Living Science Centre

MAP B1 ■ Rotunda do Ilhéu Mole ■ 291 854 274 ■ Open 10am–6pm daily ■ Adm ■ www.portomoniz.cienciaviva.pt

This cultural centre has engaging interactive exhibitions. Look out for the 3D film about the UNESCO-designated *laurissilva* forest *(see p29)*.

TOP 10 TIPS FOR FAMILIES

1 Hotels
Stay in a five-star hotel for the extra facilities, such as pools, tennis, games rooms, mini-golf and satellite TV.

2 Indulgence
Madeirans love children, so yours will get plenty of friendly attention.

3 Downtown
You can safely let older children wander on their own; crime is almost nonexistent on the island.

4 Lido Cinemas
MAP G6 ■ 291 706 800
The Forum Madeira mall *(see p77)* has a multiplex cinema. Foreign films, except animated features, are subtitled.

5 History Lesson
Learn about the island at the Madeira Story Centre *(see p23)*, which has engaging historical and cultural displays for both adults and children.

6 Playgrounds
The best playgrounds in Funchal are in the grounds of Quinta Magnólia and Jardim de Santa Catarina *(see p50)*.

7 Funchal Marina
MAP Q3
Stroll around the marina to spot fish, boats and pictures painted on the concrete walls by visiting sailors.

8 Promenade
Many families stroll along Avenida do Mar and buy snacks from the kiosks.

9 Porto Moniz
MAP B1
Known as "nature's pools", the rock pools at Port Moniz are great for bathing in warm, shallow water.

10 Porto Santo
Virtually traffic free, Porto Santo is a place to let your children off the leash to explore by bike or on foot.

Rock pools at Porto Moniz

🔟 Restaurants

Classy interior of the exclusive, Michelin-starred Il Gallo d'Oro

① Il Gallo d'Oro
Chef Benoît Sinthon's vision and technique has won this exclusive gourmet restaurant two Michelin stars. Besides an à la carte choice, diners can opt for the Signature Menu, a gastronomic treat using local and Mediterranean flavours complemented by memorable wines. Reservations essential *(see p79)*.

② William
Housed in the world-famous Reid's, William's has elegant waiting staff serving one-star Michelin cuisine under crystal chandeliers. The dress code is smart formal: gentlemen need a jacket. Book ahead as it gets busy *(see p79)*.

③ Gavião Novo
A restaurant celebrated for its exceptional (locally caught) fish and seafood menu, Gavião Novo offers authentic dining in the heart of the Zona Velha. Visitors can mix with locals who are drawn to a menu that features island favourites such as *espetada* – skewers filled with meats and poultry. The fish dishes are also excellent *(see p79)*.

④ Dona Amelia
A long-established restaurant, Dona Amelia has a favourable reputation. The chef's suggestions at this cheery eatery include delicious seafood risotto and succulent steak tartare. Dessert choices list crêpes flambés. Island and mainland wines are available and a cocktail bar for aperitifs *(see p79)*.

⑤ Vila do Peixe
Diners get a wonderful view to write home about as they sample some of the tastiest fish and seafood found in this part of the island. Try the market fish platter, slow-grilled to perfection over glowing embers. Smart and chic, the venue is a favourite with groups so check availability well ahead *(see p85)*.

⑥ La Perla
The charming 19th-century manor house Quinta Splendida houses this noted gourmet hot spot. Honoured by culinary awards, La Perla prides itself on its seasonal menu of regional and southern European dishes prepared with panache *(see p99)*.

7 Abrigo do Pastor

The rustic decor sets the theme for this atmospheric eatery. The food is rich and hearty: *javoli* (wild boar) is always on the menu. Plates of rabbit or goat stew also feature. On Sundays they serve a special, *cozida à Portuguesa* – a grand concoction of meats, potato and vegetables *(see p99)*.

8 Tasca Literária Dona Joana Rabo-de-Peixe

A quirky decor of photographs of local writers and books adds character to this delightful eatery. This is where the Art Opens Doors project *(see p22)* began, over small plates of *petiscos* (snacks) and wine *(see p79)*.

9 Cantinho da Serra

Eat here in winter and be treated to a roaring log fire at this country inn where the menu celebrates tasty Portuguese cuisine made from traditional recipes. Food is served in clay pots, lending a rustic, authentic flavour to the proceedings *(see p85)*.

10 Quinta do Furão

Known for its modern take on typical Madeiran gastronomy, this hotel-restaurant also has a vegetarian menu. The wine list links Portuguese labels with your meal. Ask for a table on the terrace, with wonderful views *(see p85)*.

Terrace tables at Quinta do Furão

TOP 10 MADEIRAN DISHES

Fish soup with tomato

1 Sopa de Tomate e Cebola
Tomato and onion soup crowned with a boiled egg and garnished with chopped parsley.

2 Açorda
Soup flavoured with garlic and coriander, made with bread and golden olive oil, topped off with a poached egg.

3 Espetada
Herb-flavoured barbecued beef, sometimes served on skewers that hang from a frame by your table.

4 Milho Frito
Deep-fried maize (like Italian polenta), traditionally served with *espetada*, though fries are now more common.

5 Lapas
Limpets, plucked from Madeira's rocky shores and grilled with garlic butter.

6 Bolo de Caco
Madeiran leavened flat-bread, baked on top of the oven and served plain or with garlic and herb butter.

7 Espada
Scabbard fish, a succulent and (usually) boneless white fish, traditionally served grilled with fried banana.

8 Prego
Delicious Madeiran fast food – grilled steak in a bread bun (*prego special* has ham and/or cheese as well).

9 Picado
Succulent pieces of beef, fried with garlic and red peppers, served up with French fries.

10 Bacalhau
Dried salted cod – very traditional, but an acquired taste, served in many ways, including with potatoes and egg, or casseroled with tomatoes and onion.

For a key to restaurant price ranges see p79

🔟 Wine Outlets

1 Blandy's Wine Lodge, Funchal

Set in a 17th-century friary, this lodge offers tastings and tours of its attics. Take a Vintage Tour for in-depth information *(see pp16–17)*.

2 Justino's, Funchal

MAP L4 ▪ Parque Industrial da Cancela, Caniço ▪ 291 934 257 ▪ www.justinosmadeira.com

Established in 1870, Justino is one of the island's oldest producers of Madeira wine. Its modern premises stock award-winning labels, including 10-year-old white grape varieties and prized vintages.

3 Artur de Barros e Sousa, Funchal

MAP N3 ▪ Rua dos Ferreiros 109 ▪ 291 220 622 ▪ Closed Sat, Sun & Aug

Known as ABS, this is one of the island's smallest producers; so small that the brothers who run it sell only to "friends" – fortunately, this includes anyone who walks in.

4 Lagar d'Ajuda, Funchal

MAP G6 ▪ Galerias Jardins da Ajuda, Estrada Monumental ▪ 291 771 551

This timbered shop set around an antique wine press has a wide range of ports, sherries and Portuguese regional wines, as well as Madeira.

Blandy's Madeira wine

5 Loja dos Vinhos, Funchal

MAP G6 ▪ Edifício Eden Mar, Loja 19, Rua do Gorgulho ▪ 291 762 869

Conveniently located in the heart of the hotel district, and open late, this wine shop sells the vintages of all of Madeira's main producers, including some rare bottles from the 19th century. They will also take telephone orders and make hotel deliveries.

6 Airport Shop, Madeira Airport

MAP K5

If you decide you cannot go home without a bottle of Madeira, the Madeira Wine Company has a duty-free shop at the airport, where you can buy 3-, 5-, 10- and 15-year-old wines, as well as a selection of single-grape, single-harvest vintage wines that are over 20 years old.

7 D'Oliveiras, Funchal

MAP N3 ▪ Rua dos Ferreiros 107 ▪ 291 220 784 ▪ Open 9am–6pm Mon–Fri, 9:30am–1pm Sat

In a timber barn with a carved stone door that bears the city's coat of arms and the date AD 1619, this wine lodge offers vintages from 1850, younger wines, miniatures and gift boxes.

Cosy interior of D'Oliveiras

(8) Henriques & Henriques, Câmara de Lobos

MAP F6 ▪ Avenida da Altonomia 10 ▪ 291 941 551 ▪ www.henriquese henriques.pt

Founded in 1850, this firm has won a string of medals and awards for dispelling the fusty image of Madeira wine and winning back a younger clientele. They introduced stylish modern labels and bottle designs, while retaining the traditional qualities of the wines themselves.

(9) Vinhos Barbeito, Câmara de Lobos

MAP F6 ▪ Estrada da Ribeira Gracia, Parque Empresarial de Câmara de Lobos ▪ 291 761 829 ▪ www. vinhosbarbeito.com

This revered Madeira wine label ages its wines in giant, iron-hooped barrels made from American oak and satinwood. Their wines include 3-, 5-, 10- and special 20-year-old bottles and Reserves.

Vineyards at Vinhos Barbeito

(10) Quinta do Furão, Santana

MAP H2 ▪ Estada Quinta do Furão 6, Santana ▪ 291 570 100 ▪ www. quintadofurao.com

This hotel, restaurant and wine shop belonging to the Madeira Wine Company is set amid extensive vineyards near Santana, in the north of the island. Visitors can follow lovely trails through the vineyards, and help with the harvest during late summer and early autumn. In the wine cellar you can taste and buy four types of Madeira wine *(see p85)*.

TOP 10 MADEIRAN WINE TERMS

Bottles of Madeira wine

1 Sercial
The driest of the traditional Madeira wines. Excellent aperitif or with soup.

2 Verdelho
A tawny, medium dry wine good for drinking with food.

3 Bual/Boal
A nutty dessert wine ideal with cheese or puddings.

4 Malmsey/Malvasia
The richest and sweetest Madeira wine, best for after-dinner drinking.

5 Dry, Medium Dry and Medium Sweet
These wines are three years old, and made from *tinta negra mole* grapes. They lack the depth of real Madeira.

6 Estufagem
The process of ageing the wine in casks kept in an *estufa* (hothouse), or of heating the wine in tanks to make it age even faster. The second method yields inferior results.

7 Canteiro
The term *canteiro* is used to distinguish quality wines and is a slow method of ageing Madeira in casks heated naturally by the sun.

8 Reserve
A blend of wines made by the two methods of *estufagem* and with an average age of five years. Made mostly with *tinta negra mole* grapes.

9 Special Reserve
A blend of wines aged in casks for about ten years. They are usually made with the noble grape varieties (1–4 above).

10 Vintage Wines
The finest Madeira, aged for a minimum of 20 years in casks and a further two years in the bottle.

Specialist Shops

1 Jardins Quinta da Boa Vista, Funchal

MAP H5 ▪ Rua do Lombo da Boa Vista 25 ▪ 291 220 468 ▪ Open 9am–5:30pm Mon–Sat ▪ Adm

Boa Vista specialize in brightly coloured bromeliads ("air plants"), but also grow and sell a great range of other exotic plants *(see p51)*.

Orchids growing at Boa Vista Orchids

2 Armazém do Mercado, Funchal

The "Warehouse Market" is filled with pop-up boutiques selling a range of products that are ideal for gifts or souvenirs, from handmade trinkets to locally produced wine and various foodstuffs *(see p23)*.

3 Fado and Folk

The late-night café-music of Portuguese *fado* can become addictive. The best place to find the latest CDs by the superstars Ana Moura, Mariza, Mísia and Madredeus is the FNAC music and book store in the Madeira Shopping complex *(see p77)*, which is located on the outskirts of Funchal.

4 Leather Goods

Pele Leather: MAP P3; Rua das Murças 26A, Funchal; 291 223 619

There are fashionable leather shops aplenty in the narrow streets that lie north and south of Funchal Cathedral *(see pp12–13)*, but a factory outlet called Pele Leather has some of the best value leather goods on offer.

5 Patricio & Gouveia, Funchal

MAP P4 ▪ Rua Visconde de Anadia 34 ▪ 291 220 801

Tour the embroidery factory to find out how traditional designs are transferred from parchment to linen, before browsing the shop for blouses, tablecloths and nightgowns with beautiful antique lace.

6 Cakes and Pastries

Penha d'Águia: MAP P3; Rua das Murças 21 ▪ A Lua: MAP P2; Rua da Carreira 78.

For delicious *pastéis de nata* (custard tarts) for immediate consumption, or *bolo de mel* (honey cake) or *amêndoa torrão* (almond sweetmeats) that will survive the journey home, try Penha d'Águia or A Lua.

7 O Relógio, Camacha

Packed to the ceiling with furniture, plant pots, baskets, toys and lampshades, this Aladdin's cave of wicker scarcely has any room to move. If you catch one of the interesting demonstrations of wickerwork, you'll see nimble fingers making the bending and weaving of willow canes look much easier than it really is *(see p66)*.

Wicker gifts at O Relógio in Camacha

Lace embroidery at Casa do Turista

⑧ Casa do Turista, Funchal
MAP Q2 ■ Rua do Conselheiro José Silvestre Ribeiro 2 ■ 291 224 907 ■ Open 9:30am–6:30pm Mon–Fri, till 1pm Sat

This shop is located in the elegant 19th-century former townhouse of the German consul. The "Tourist House" boasts a full range of Portuguese-made silver, ceramics, glassware and linen (see p77).

⑨ Livraria Esperança, Funchal

Even if you can't read Portuguese, Livraria Esperança is well worth a visit. Filling an old palace, Portugal's biggest bookstore is charmingly old-fashioned. There are volumes on every theme possible here, from children's books to brain-surgery manuals. Alongside these are a few titles in English (see p77).

⑩ Barros e Abreu, Funchal
MAP Q5 ■ Rua do Portão de São Tiago 20–22

The traditional leather ankle boots made by Barros e Abreu Irmãos are surprisingly comfortable, but unlike their beautiful and timeless leather sandals, they may look out of place back home. See them being made at the workshop in the Zona Velha. The best time to drop by is during the early evening.

TOP 10 GIFTS TO BUY

1 Embroidery
Now highly regarded by couturiers, Madeiran embroidery had unlikely beginnings; it was started by Bella Phelps in 1844 to provide work during a slump in the wine trade.

2 Tapestry
A close cousin of embroidery, tapestry has been produced on the island ever since the 1890s. Kits are available for amateur enthusiasts.

3 Wicker
Centred around Camacha, Madeira's wickerworkers create at least 1,200 different articles.

4 Wine and Liqueurs
As well as fortified Madeira wine, the island produces *poncha*, a potent blend of sugarcane rum, honey and lemon juice.

5 Leather
Bags and shoes made of leather are a Portuguese speciality.

6 Pottery
Another speciality is pottery in Moorish designs, or shaped like cabbage leaves.

7 Cakes
Festive *bolo de mel* (honey cake), once made only at Christmas, is now a year-round treat, made using cane sugar, nuts and fruit.

8 Flowers
Colourful and long-lasting blooms are a good souvenir of this garden isle.

9 Boots and Sandals
These are handmade in raw leather, to a timeless design.

10 Pompom Hats
Thick, cable-knit hats and sweaters made from raw undyed wool are worn by Madeira's farmers to keep off the chill during the cooler months.

Traditional embroidered ornament

Madeira For Free

Viewing platform at Cabo Girão

① Cabo Girão
At 580 m (1,903 ft), the highest sea cliff in Madeira is impressive. The viewing platform at the top gives a dizzying panorama below – because the floor is made of glass – as well as out across the cliff edge. If you suffer from vertigo, don't even think about venturing on to it (see p81).

② Mercado dos Lavradores
Arrive early and browse the fruit and vegetable stalls on the ground floor of the market. You may be offered a free slice of mango or custard apple to try. Afterwards, head for the basement and the busy fish market. Upstairs, look for the wines and liqueurs – free tastings are not uncommon (see pp24–5).

③ O Relógio, Camacha
MAP J5 ■ Largo Conselheiro Aires de Ornelas 12, Camacha ■ 291 922 777 ■ Open 8:45am–6pm daily ■ www.caferelogio.com
Housed in a building named O Relógio (meaning "the Clock") this wicker factory is where visitors can watch free demonstrations of wicker-making and appreciate the craftsmanship involved. Lampshades, baskets and wine-bottle holders are examples of the sorts of items made and sold here (see p97).

④ Funchal Cathedral (Sé)
The plain exterior of Funchal's cathedral belies an extraordinarily rich interior of paintings, statues and gilded chapels. The highlight is the knotwork ceiling, one of the richest and most elaborate in Portugal, which blends Moorish and European design elements (see pp12–13).

⑤ Igreja do Colégio Guided Walking Tour
MAP P3 ■ Rua dos Ferreiros 11, Funchal ■ 291 705 060 ■ Open 10am– 6pm Mon–Fri; 3–6pm Sat; 9am–1pm, 6:30– 8:30pm Sun ■ www.colegiodos jesuitas.pt
The ornate basalt façade of this 17th-century Jesuit church is a treat. The interior has finely detailed fres- coes, gilded filigree carvings and rare glazed tiles, design hallmarks of the Jesuit brotherhood. The old school buildings now form part of the University of Madeira and can be explored on a guided tour (see p46).

⑥ Traditional Santana Houses
MAP H2 ■ Rua do Sacristão, Santana ■ 10am–6pm daily
These wonderful A-frame houses, with their scarlet doors and square windows, are endearingly compact and cosy. The island's tourist-board examples in Santana have been immaculately preserved within trim gardens, their thatched roofs and painted doorways still in pristine condition (see p82).

Traditional Santana house

⑦ Frente Mar and the Jardim Panorâmico

MAP G6 ▪ Estrada Monumental, Funchal

The seafront esplanade from the Lido district all the way to Praia Formosa *(see pp52–3)* makes for a pleasant walk, with bars, cafés and restaurants along the way. Linger in the terraced Jardim Panorâmico, an appealing suntrap with coastal views.

⑧ Fortaleza de São Tiago

The São Tiago fortress marks the boundary of the Zona Velha. Built to repel pirate attack, the stronghold is a good place for kids to run about. The views out across the Atlantic are stupendous, and there are a couple of good places to eat in and around the building. Ideal for a day trip.

⑨ Capela do Corpo Santo

This simple chapel in the Zona Velha was built in the 15th century, though what you see today is largely 16th century. It was made by a charity that raised funds for local fishermen and their families, who didn't have enough money to buy food or take shelter *(see pp22–3)*.

⑩ Palácio de São Lourenço Guided Walking Tour

Dating from 1513, this beautiful fortress-palace was the residence of Madeira's military island governors up to 1834. Its rooms brim with Portuguese and European decorative art, and there is also an exhibition about the fort's history *(see p76)*. The walking tour is suitable for all levels of fitness.

TOP 10 MONEY-SAVING TIPS

Porto Santo Line ferry

1 Discounted Entrance Prices
Look for savings on family, group and senior citizen (+65) tickets, and discounts for children at attractions.

2 Porto Santo Restaurants
Several restaurants on the island offer a free taxi service for clients to and from their hotels *(see p105)*.

3 International Museum Day
International Museum Day falls every year on May 18, when all museums are free to enter.

4 Airport Shuttle Bus
MAP Q3 ▪ www.sam.pt
The SAM Aerobus runs between the airport and Funchal city centre and is far cheaper than any taxi.

5 Free Island Guide
Look for the free Best of Madeira Guide at hotels and restaurants: it's full of discount vouchers for various services.

6 Porto Santo Ferry
www.portosantoline.pt
Check the Porto Santo Line website for round-trip ticket offers in Apr–Sept.

7 Combined Cable Car Ticket
MAP P5 ▪ www.madeiracablecar.com
Purchase a combined return ticket to visit Monte *(see pp34–5)* and Jardim Botânico *(see pp26–7)*.

8 Use a Prepaid Giro Card
www.horariosdofunchal.pt
Buy a rechargeable Giro card and load it with trips for Funchal bus travel *(see pp108–9)*.

9 Happy Hour
Note "happy hour" times posted outside bars in resorts. Enjoy the savings but drink and behave responsibly.

10 All Inclusive
Many hotels offer all inclusive packages including entertainment, drinks and meals, though this can feel restrictive.

TOP 10 Festivals

1 Carnival
Funchal ■ Feb–Mar (47 days before Easter)

Celebrated over three days before Shrove Tuesday, Carnival is when schools, clubs and bands parade down the streets in fancy dress, followed by a colourful allegorical parade on the last day. Not as wild as Rio, but still an excuse to let your hair down.

Glamorous carnival costumes

2 Flower Festival
Funchal ■ Apr/May

The floats come out again for the spring Flower Festival in April or May. This was originally created as a tourist attraction, but now it is a festival that Madeirans have taken to their heart, with passionate competition among local clubs to produce the best float.

Pretty float at the Flower Festival

3 Atlantic Festival
Funchal ■ Jun

Held throughout June, the Festival do Atlântico combines fireworks, street entertainment and a music festival. There are performances by international stars as well as the accomplished local musicians from the Orquestra Clássica da Madeira, the Orquestra de Mandolins and the Funchal Brass Ensemble.

4 Jazz Festival
Funchal ■ First week of Jul

Staged in Santa Catarina Park (see p50), this prestigious three-day event, held in the first week of July, attracts some of the most famous names in international jazz, such as Jean Luc Ponty and Kenny Garret. Musicians include artists from Madeira and mainland Portugal. Jam sessions are staged at venues around Funchal to accompany the main programme.

5 Assumption in Monte
Monte, Funchal ■ 15 Aug

The Virgin is greatly revered by pious Madeirans because they believe she takes pity on human suffering. The day on which the Virgin is believed to have been assumed into heaven, 15 August, is observed in Monte (see pp34–5) with religious services and elaborate processions by day, and feasting, live music and a lot of dancing by night.

⑥ Columbus Festival
Vila Baleira ■ Early Sep

Costumed parades, street theatre, concerts and exhibitions in Porto Santo's tiny capital, Vila Baleira *(see p101)*, re-create Columbus's arrival.

⑦ Feast of Bom Jesus
Ponta Delgada ■ First Sun of Sep

Pilgrims from all over the island come to Ponta Delgada *(see p84)* during this important religious festival to pray to the Bom Jesus ("Good Jesus"), a Christ figure believed to have miraculous powers.

⑧ Wine Festival
Estreito de Câmara de Lobos ■ Mid-Sep

The grape harvest is celebrated in Estreito de Câmara de Lobos with folk music and demonstrations of grape-crushing done with bare feet.

Crushing grapes at the Wine Festival

⑨ Nature Festival
Funchal ■ Second week of Oct

This festival promotes Madeira's natural resources and the best way to experience them on land, on sea or in the air. The initiative links sports and outdoor activities with ethnography and Madeiran culture.

⑩ Christmas and New Year
Throughout ■ Dec

In December churches and shops mount cribs filled with traditional figures, such as rustic shepherds. The New Year's Eve fireworks have been recognized by Guinness Book of Records as the world's largest.

TOP 10 FESTIVE TRADITIONS

Typical *bolo de caco* bread

1 Bolo de Caco
Barbecued kebabs are eaten with spongy *bolo de caco* bread, a soft leavened flatbread, baked on the top of a stone oven.

2 Barbecues
No village festival is complete without delicious beef kebabs, barbecued in an old oil barrel.

3 Wine
Festivals are also a chance to sample local wines (and cider) that are not sold commercially.

4 Street Decorations
When streets are turned into tunnels of flowers, it's a sure sign that a festival is on the way.

5 Festive Greenery
Flower garlands are hung from poles wrapped in branches of sweet bay.

6 Flags and Light Bulbs
Bright white bulbs light up the night, and Madeira's flag – a red cross on a white background – is everywhere.

7 Firecrackers
Exploding firecrackers mark the start of a village festival (or a victory by one of the local football teams).

8 Processions and Sermons
Before the fun begins, the serious bit: a religious service to honour the patron saint.

9 Wall of Hope
At the Flower Festival, children make a wish and pin posies to a board in front of the town hall.

10 Music and Dance
Bands known as *filarmónicas*, which are formed of brass, accordian and wind instruments, provide the music for dancing the night away.

Madeira
Area by Area

Striking views over the cliffs from
Ponta de São Lourenço

🔟 Funchal

Founded in 1425, Funchal was granted city status in 1508. Many of its finest historical buildings are still intact, despite floods, piracy and earthquakes. Named Funchal ("Fennel") because of the wild fennel plants found growing in abundance by the first settlers, Madeira's capital sits on the island's southern coast in a natural amphitheatre, hemmed in by cliffs to the east and west, and steep green mountains to the north. Its streets are paved with black-and-white mosaics, and lined by blue-flowered jacaranda trees. Numerous public parks and private gardens make this a festive city filled with heady scents and colours, where architecture and nature are delightfully combined.

Leda and the Swan in the Town Hall courtyard

FUNCHAL

1 **Top 10 Sights**
see pp72–75

1 **Places to Eat**
see p79

1 **The Best of the Rest**
see p76

1 **Places to Shop**
see p77

1 **Nights Out**
see p78

1 Around the Town Hall
MAP P3

Chic clothing shops line the narrow pedestrian streets that stretch up in a grid from the cathedral to the city's only open square, with its fountain and fish-scale-patterned paving. The square is framed by the graceful Baroque Câmara Municipal (Town Hall) *(see p44)* and the pretty Bishop's Palace, now the Museu de Arte Sacra (Museum of Sacred Art) *(see pp14–15)*.

Atmospheric streets, Zona Velha

2 Zona Velha
MAP P5

Funchal was the first Portuguese city to be founded outside the traditional boundaries of Europe, and the Zona Velha *(see pp22–3)* is where it all began. The original settlement was protected by the Fortaleza de São Tiago. Today, restaurants and bars line the rejuvenated Rua de Santa Maria and cluster around the Capela do Corpo Santo *(see p23)*. A seafront promenade and park link the Zona Velha to the Monte cable car station *(see p35)* and the covered Mercado dos Lavradores *(see pp24–5)*. The Zona Velha also houses the Madeira Story Centre *(see p23)*.

CALÇADA PAVEMENTS

The pavements of Funchal are works of art. Blocks of dove-grey basalt and creamy limestone are laid in intricate mosaic patterns, from the fish-scale design of the Town Hall square to the heraldic and floral motifs along Avenida Arriaga. Along Rua João Tavira, north of the cathedral, the mosaics depict the city's coat of arms – a wine carrier and the ship that brought Zarco (see p19).

Carmo Quarter
MAP N4

The Carmo Quarter lies between two of the three creeks that flow through Funchal. Their deep channels across the city were once overhung with purple and red bougainvillea. Linking the 17th-century Carmo Church, the Franco Museum (see p48) and IBTAM is a warren of narrow streets, with fine buildings like the House of the Consuls (see p44).

São Pedro and Santa Clara
MAP N2

North of Rua da Carreira lie some of the best museums in Funchal. The Museu Municipal (see p49) in Rua Mouraria has a pretty herb garden beside it, and the church of São Pedro (see p46) is lined with lovely 17th-century tiles. The steep Calçada de Santa Clara leads to the Freitas Museum (see p48), Santa Clara Convent (see pp20–21) and the Quinta das Cruzes Museum (see pp18–19).

Interior of the church of São Pedro

5 Cathedral Quarter
MAP P3

When Christopher Columbus visited his friend João Esmeraldo in 1498, the cathedral (see pp12–13) and the Alfândega (Customs House) (see p42) were still being built. Esmeraldo's home later became the City of Sugar Museum, and the Customs House, near the sociable pavement cafés surrounding the cathedral, has become Madeira's regional parliament building.

6 University Quarter
MAP N2

Statues of Jesuit saints stand in niches in the façade of the Igreja do Colégio (see p46), the huge and ornate church whose ancient school buildings are now the administrative offices of the University of Madeira (see p45). On the six city blocks to the north and on either side of these offices, you will find old-fashioned bookshops, cobbled wine lodges (see p62) and some of the city's oldest and most ornate tower houses.

7 Rua da Carreira
MAP P2

Funchal was once known as "Little Lisbon", and the elegant buildings on Rua da Carreira, with their green shutters and iron balconies hung with plants, are a taste of the Portuguese capital. At the western end, a pretty casa de prazer (garden gazebo) sits on the corner of Rua do Quebra Costas, the street that leads to the secluded gardens of the Igreja Inglesa (English Church) (see p44).

8 Seafront and Marina
MAP Q3

Everything in Funchal looks out to the sparkling sea and busy harbour, where private yachts, container ships and cruise liners on transatlantic voyages call in. Damaged by floods in 2010, the port and marina have been undergoing redevelopment ever since (see p43). Stroll along Avenida do Mar in the sunshine, and sample coffee and cakes at the kiosks along the seafront.

Yachts moored in Funchal's marina

9 Around Avenida Arriaga
MAP P2

Wide and leafy Avenida Arriaga is lined with some of Funchal's most prestigious public buildings. On the north side are the offices of the regional government, the Bank of Portugal building (see p45), Blandy's Wine Lodge (see pp16–17), the tourist office, the art gallery and the São Francisco Gardens. On the south side is the huge São Lourenço fortress (see p76), the Ritz Restaurant with its tiled exterior (see p45), several good shopping arcades (see p77) and the theatre (see p78) and its chic café.

10 Hotel Zone
MAP Q1

West of the city, a succession of parks (see p50) and Art Deco mansions from the 1920s and 1930s line the Avenida do Infante. As the road crosses the ravine of the Ribeira Seco ("Dry River") and curves past Reid's Palace (see p114), mansions give way to big hotels along the clifftops, along with shopping centres and restaurants.

A DAY IN OLD FUNCHAL

▶ **MORNING**

Arrive for around 9am at **Mercado dos Lavradores** (see pp24–5), perhaps for a coffee and *bolo de caco* (see p61) at the rooftop Macaronésia café, before heading downstairs to the market.

Next, head for the **Madeira Story Centre** (see p23) for an overview of the island and its history and culture. While you're in this area you can explore the **Zona Velha** (see pp22–5) and wander the Jardim do Almirante Reis. Afterwards double back until you reach the **Funchal Cathedral** (see pp12–13). This will introduce you to the two main styles of Madeiran church architecture: both 16th-century Gothic and 18th-century Baroque.

For a break or a bite to eat, enjoy Funchal's laid-back café life in one of the eateries on Rua João Tavira and Rua da Sé.

AFTERNOON

Walk off your lunch by strolling along **Avenida Arriaga** until the Jardim Município. From here it's anuphill amble along Calçada de Santa Clara to the **Museu da Quinta das Cruzes** (see pp18–19). Allow at least an hour to explore the museum and its leafy archaeological gardens. Visit the neighbouring **Convento de Santa Clara** (see pp20–21). On the way back down you'll pass the engaging **Freitas Museum** (see p48), which is worth half an hour.

Arrive back on Avenida Arriaga before 4:30pm for a guided tour of **Blandy's Wine Lodge** (see pp16–17), with wine tastings.

See map on pp72–73 ←

Best of the Rest

1 Fortaleza do Pico
MAP N1 ■ **Rua do Castelo** ■
Open 9am–6pm Mon–Sat

It's an uphill slog from the centre to this undervisited fortress, but the views across the city are worth it. Still partly used by the military, but certain parts are open to the public.

2 Casa da Luz – Museu de Electricidade

This former power station explores the heroic efforts that were needed to bring electricity to the island. Some of the huge machinery required is on display (see p22).

3 Núcleo Museológico do Bordado

MAP N4 ■ **Rua do Visconde do Anadia 44** ■ **291 211 600** ■ **www.bordado madeira.pt** ■ Open 9:30am–12:30pm & 2–5:30pm Mon–Fri ■ Adm

The history of Madeira's embroidery, tapestry and handicrafts, including the island's colourful costumes.

4 Art Opens Doors

This project has meant that the doors in Madeira's oldest street have been decorated with striking designs. The work was carried out by a range of local and international artists in a variety of styles (see p22).

5 Palácio de São Lourenço
MAP P3 ■ **Avenida Zarco** ■ **291 202 530** ■ Guided tours 12:30pm Mon, 10am Tue–Wed, 10am & 12:30pm Thu, 3pm Fri

The historic fortress has displays on the French pirate Bertrand de Montluc (see p36).

6 History Tellers
MAP P4 ■ **Armazém do Mercado, Rua Latino Coelho 39** ■ **291 705 060** ■ **www.historytellers.pt**

Informative walking tours recounting Madeira's colourful past, led by students from the University of Madeira.

7 Museu Bordado e do Artesanto

MAP N4 ■ **Rua Visconde de Anadia 44, Funchal** ■ **291 211 600** ■ 9:30am–12:30pm, 2–5pm Mon–Fri ■ Adm

Some delicate embroidery from the mid-19th century to the 1930s is on display here, along with rare furniture.

8 Madeira Film Experience

MAP Q2 ■ **Marina Shopping, Rua Conselheiro José Silvestre 1** ■ **291 222 748** ■ Open 10am–5:45pm daily ■ **www.madeirafilmexperience.com**

This packs 600 years of history and culture into an entertaining, 30-minute audiovisual experience

9 Museu do Brinquedo

From 19th-century china dolls to 1980s plastic Barbies, this has over 100 years of toy history, with a huge collection of miniature cars. There is a ground-floor restaurant (see p22).

10 Universo de Memórias
MAP N2 ■ **Santa Clara Civic and Cultural Centre, Calçada do Pico 2** ■ **291 225 122** ■ Open 10am–5pm Tue–Sat ■ Adm

A thought-provoking exhibition of memorabilia collected by traveller, writer, politician and artist João Carlos Abreu.

Palacio de São Lourenço

Places to Shop

1 Madeira Shopping
MAP G5 ■ Caminho de Santa Quitéria 45, Santo António
Providing retail therapy for serious shopaholics, this huge shopping mall features top brands in over 100 stores. Follow signs from the São Martinho exit of the Via Rapida, or take the Horários do Funchal bus 8 from the city centre.

2 Casa do Turista
All the elegance of a bygone era is here: Madeiran and mainland Portuguese textiles, ceramics, silver and glassware displayed in a stately townhouse (see p65).

3 Galerias São Lourenço
MAP P2 ■ Avenida Arriaga 41
Funchal's most upmarket shopping mall, offering everything from sunglasses and children's clothes to elegant kitchen- and tableware.

4 Armazém do Mercado
This is a series of pop-up local business enterprises. Visitors can shop for organic produce as well as quirky souvenirs (see p23). There are a number of quality eateries located here, too.

5 La Vie Shopping Centre
MAP P1 ■ Rua Dr Brito Câmara 9
This modern temple to consumerism boasts eye-catching architecture and a city centre location. It houses a plethora of fashion boutiques, jewellers, leisurewear and sports shops, as well as a hypermarket.

6 Design Center Nini Andrade Silva
MAP H6 ■ Estrada da Pontinha, Forte de Nossa Senhora da Conceição ■ 291 648 780 ■ Open 10am–7pm daily ■ www.niniandradesilva.com
Funchal-born interior designer Nini Andrade Silva has created several Madeira hotel interiors. Here her work is showcased alongside a smart restaurant.

Mercado dos Lavradores

7 Mercado dos Lavradores
Make it a habit while in Funchal to visit the market and shop for picnic ingredients or souvenirs, or to savour the colourful bustle (see pp24–5).

8 Livraria Esperança
MAP N3 ■ Rua dos Ferreiros 119 ■ 291 221 118 ■ Open 9am–7pm Mon–Fri
A cavernous homage to all things literary, this claims to be Portugal's largest bookshop with over 100,000 new and secondhand titles. Seek out the good foreign-language section.

9 Forum Madeira
MAP G6 ■ Estrada Monumental 390, Lido
This stylish mall houses over 80 stores, a giant hypermarket, 17 restaurants and six cinemas. Sea views can be enjoyed from the rooftop terrace.

10 Rua Dr. Fernão Ornelas
MAP P4
Funchal's main shopping street is a wonderful mix of chic boutiques sitting cheek-by-jowl with grocers selling coffee and pungent salt cod. Most shops close on Saturday afternoon and Sunday.

See map on pp72–73

Nights Out

Exterior of 23 Vintage Bar

1 23 Vintage
MAP Q6 ▪ Rua de Santa Maria 27 ▪ 291 630 339 ▪ Open 8pm–2am

In Funchal's old town, this fashionable late-night bar is a popular local spot, with music of the 1970s, 80s and 90s.

2 Venda Velha
MAP Q6 ▪ Rua de Santa Maria 170 ▪ 925 003 460 ▪ Open noon–4am daily; winter hours may vary

Madeira's potent tipple, *poncha (see p65)*, is served with gusto at this bar. On Friday and Saturday nights, the revelry spills out on to the terrace.

3 Teatro Municipal
MAP P2 ▪ Avenida Arriaga ▪ 291 215 130

This resplendent theatre (built 1888) hosts music recitals, contemporary dance, drama (usually in Portuguese) as well as art-house movies. Look for billboards outside the theatre telling you what's on.

4 Café do Teatro
MAP P2 ▪ Avenida Arriaga 40 ▪ 291 226 371

The romantic night-time haunt of Funchal's smart set, this small but sophisticated café offers cocktails, chat and occasional DJs.

5 Scat Funchal Jazz Club
MAP G6 ▪ Promenade do Lido ▪ 291 775 927

Enjoy live jazz concerts by national and international performers at this bar/restaurant.

6 Discoteca Vespas
MAP Q2 ▪ Avenida Sá Carneiro 7 (opposite the container port) ▪ 291 234 800

At Madeira's best-known disco, three clubs under the same roof cater to a youthful crowd of locals and tourists.

7 Sabor a Fado
MAP P5 ▪ Travessa das Torres 10 ▪ 925 612 259

Pleasant restaurant with live music by the waiting staff and an authentic and traditional Portuguese menu.

8 Casino da Madeira
MAP H6 ▪ Avenida do Infante ▪ 291 140 424 ▪ Open 3pm–3am Sun–Thu, 4pm–4am Fri, Sat and bank holidays ▪ www.casinoda madeira.com

Play slot machines, roulette and blackjack at this casino, or enjoy the spectacular dinner shows and live music in the Copacabana Bar.

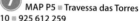

Casino da Madeira

9 Living Room
MAP P3 ▪ Travessa dos Varadouros 4-8 ▪ 965 366 207 ▪ 11pm–4am Fri–Sat

Funky boutique bar and dance club that's also an art gallery. Local DJs work in this micro space that's also a decent gin palace.

10 Classical Concerts
MAP P1 ▪ English Church: Rua Quebra Costas 18 ▪ 291 752 173 ▪ www.orquestradebandolinsdamadeira.net

The Mandolin Orchestra plays at the English Church on Friday nights (not August). For Orquestra Clássica and the Brass Ensemble, see posters.

➤ *See map on pp72–73*

Places to Eat

1 **Armazém do Sal**
MAP P3 ▪ Rua da Alfândega 135 ▪ 919 134 411 ▪ Closed Sun ▪ €€
Once used for storing salt, this former warehouse has been carefully transformed into a highly regarded upscale eatery. The smoked sea bass is excellent.

2 Gavião Novo
MAP Q6 ▪ Rua de Santa Maria 131, Funchal ▪ 291 229 238 ▪ €€
Celebrated for its fish and seafood, the restaurant also offers creative meat dishes such as the fillet steak with Roquefort cheese (see p60).

3 Riso Risottoria del Mundo
MAP Q6 ▪ Rua de Santa Maria 274 ▪ 291 280 360 ▪ Closed Mon ▪ €€€
Offering ocean views, this eatery is all about rice, from paella to risotto, with dishes such as green asparagus risotto with grilled scallops and hazelnut pesto.

Il Gallo d'Oro

4 Dona Amélia
MAP Q1 ▪ Rua Imperatriz Dona Amélia 83 ▪ 291 225 784 ▪ €€€
Fine-dining restaurant serving classic regional and Mediterranean dishes. Booking is advisable (see p60).

5 Restaurante do Forte
MAP Q6 ▪ Rua Portão São Tiago ▪ 291 215 580 ▪ €€€
Upmarket but informal, this romantic restaurant, set within the walls of the 17th-century Fortaleza de São Tiago, serves up excellent Portuguese cuisine, with set menus offering great value to diners.

6 UVA
MAP P2 ▪ Vine Hotel, Rua dos Aranhas 27 ▪ 291 009 000 ▪ €€
Top-notch gastronomy with top-floor views, this hotel restaurant is also a wine bar. Quality and service are both prompt and accomplished.

7 Tasca Literária Dona Joana Rabo-de-Peixe
MAP P5 ▪ Rua de Santa Maria 77 ▪ 291 220 348 ▪ Open 11am–midnight Sun–Thu, till 2pm Fri–Sat ▪ €€
Try the Guacamole à "Remelico" at this quirky tapas bar (see p61).

8 Il Gallo d'Oro
MAP G6 ▪ Cliff Bay Hotel, Estrada Monumental 147 ▪ 291 707 700 ▪ Dinner only ▪ €€€
This sophisticated dining venue has two Michelin stars (see p60).

9 William
MAP G6 ▪ Reid's Palace, Estrada Monumental 139 ▪ 291 717 171 ▪ Closed Sun & Mon, dinner only ▪ €€€
A Michelin star shines over this gourmet restaurant with fabulous ocean views (see p60).

10 Beef and Wines
MAP H6 ▪ Edifício Infante Dom Henrique 60, Avenida do Infante ▪ 291 282 257 ▪ Open noon–midnight daily ▪ €€€
Brazilian dishes picanha (grilled rump of beef) and feijoada (black-bean stew), some fish and seafood.

Interior of Beef and Wines

TOP 10 Central Madeira

The centre of Madeira consists mainly of high volcanic peaks and deep ravines. To experience this scenery to the full, it is best to walk, but thanks to well-placed *miradouros* (scenic viewing points), you can take some memorable photographs and enjoy the visual appeal of the central mountain range even when travelling by road. There are great contrasts between the north and south. Soaked in sunshine, the southern slopes are densely populated, with red-tiled farmhouses in a sea of vines and bananas. The northern slopes are densely wooded; along the coastal strip, tiny terraces cling to the steep valley sides.

Traditional home, Santana

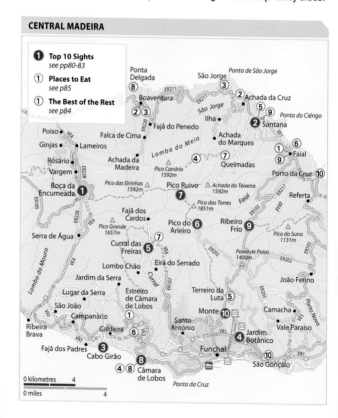

CENTRAL MADEIRA

- ❶ **Top 10 Sights**
  see pp80-83
- ① **Places to Eat**
  see p85
- ① **The Best of the Rest**
  see p84

0 kilometres 4
0 miles 4

Boca da Encumeada

The Encumeada Pass is a saddle of rock dividing the north and south of the island. Clouds from the north often spill over the tips of the mountains like dry ice pouring from a flask. There are majestic peaks, from Pico Grande in the east to cone-shaped Crista de Galo in the west. Just south of the pass is the Levada do Norte *(see pp54–5).*

Santana
MAP H2 ▪ **Horários do Funchal bus 56, Carros de São Gonçalo bus 103**

Santana has Madeira's best examples of the traditional timber-and-thatch dwellings known as *palheiros*. These brightly-painted triangular houses are comfortable but compact, and many now have modern extensions to accommodate the kitchens and bathrooms that the originals lacked. You can visit a row of tourist-board houses next to the church, but in the lanes of the village you will see plenty more, with very tidy gardens.

Cabo Girão
MAP E5 ▪ **Rodoeste bus 154**

Madeira's highest sea cliff, 580 m (1,903 ft) above the ocean, also claims to be the second highest in the world. From the glass-floored viewing point, you gaze down on to a *fajã*, a rock platform created when the cliff face fell into the sea millennia ago. Local farmers cultivate crops here in neat terraces. For a closer look, take the cable car *(teleférico)* from Caldeira Rancho, on the western side of Câmara de Lobos, to the base of the cliff.

Jardim Botânico

Come here to satisfy your curiosity about the names and origins of all the flowering trees, palms, succulents and scented climbers that grow everywhere in Madeira – in front gardens of houses, in public parks and along country roads *(see pp26–7).*

Topiary, Madeira Botanical Garden

Curral das Freiras

A long road-tunnel now links the valley village of Curral das Freiras with the wider world, the old road having been closed due to safety concerns. Upon arrival in "Nun's Refuge", you gain a sense of just how isolated this community once was *(see pp36–7).*

Curral das Freiras

6 Pico do Arieiro

In the colourful landscape of Madeira's third highest peak, you can read the story of the volcanic forces that created the island, and the elemental battles between wind, rock and rain that eroded it into the jagged peaks and plunging ravines that visitors see today *(see pp38–9)*.

Hiking path, Pico do Arieiro

7 Pico Ruivo

MAP G3 ■ No bus

Madeira's highest peak is reached from the road next to the petrol station on the eastern side of Santana. This leads to the car park at Achada do Teixeira, from where a well-paved path climbs to the summit (1,862 m/ 6,109 ft). To the south, the views look over the high peaks and jagged

A-FRAME HOUSES

The colourful A-frame houses of the Santana district were probably introduced by early settlers from the farming districts of central Portugal. Today, they are used as houses, or as cattle byres. On an island of precipitous slopes, cattle can easily fall if left to graze freely, so they are kept in the cool shade of the thatched *palheiros*, to which their owners carry stacks of freshly cut grass and foliage at regular intervals during the day *(see p66)*.

ridges of an arid volcanic landscape; to the north, clouds hang around the lush, forested slopes. Back at the car park, look out for the eroded rocks called Homem em Pé ("Standing Man") that can be seen in a hollow behind the rest house.

8 Câmara de Lobos

MAP F6 ■ All Rodoeste buses call here

The *lobos* ("wolves") in the name of this pretty village refer to the monk seals that once basked on the pebbly beach. This area is now used as an open-air boatyard, where traditional craft are repaired or given a fresh coat of blue, red and yellow paint, laid on in bold stripes. Down among the noisy bars is the Fishermen's Chapel, where villagers give thanks for the safe return of their men after a long night at sea, fishing for *espada* (scabbard fish), most of which is served up on the tables of Madeira's many restaurants. Admire the bay from Pico da Torre or continue to Estreito de Câmara de Lobos.

Harbour and colourful boats at Câmara de Lobos

9 Ribeiro Frio

MAP H4 ■ São Roque do Faial
■ Horários do Funchal bus 56, Carros
de São Gonçalo bus 103

This valley clearing's "Cold River"
tumbles down the mountain to bring
clear water to a trout farm in a pretty
garden. Some of the trout end up on
the menu of the Restaurante Ribeiro
Frio opposite, a good place to begin or
end a short walk along the dry *levada*
to Balcões. The longer Levada do
Furado walk to Portela starts here
too; you need a map to do the whole
route, but you can enjoy views of the
UNESCO-listed *laurissilva* forest in
the surrounding Ribeiro Frio Forest
Park by doing just the first stretch.

Clear waters of the Ribeiro Frio

10 Monte

Take the cable car up from
Funchal's Zona Velha to Monte, and
you will sail 600 m (1,968 ft) up the
southern face of Madeira to a place
that seems more garden than village,
shaded by veteran trees and watered
by natural springs *(see pp34–5)*.

A DAY IN CENTRAL MADEIRA

▶ MORNING

Starting in **Monte** by 10am at the
latest, head first to the summit of
Pico do Arieiro (if it's too cloudy,
do the trip in reverse; the weather
may clear later on).

Afterwards, descend to **Ribeiro
Frio** to visit the trout farm and
enjoy the native Madeiran flowers
in the surrounding gardens.

Walk downhill past the shop, and
take the *levada* path signposted
left to **Balcões** *(see p55)*. A pretty
20-minute stroll through woodland brings you to a cutting in the
rock which gives you wonderful
views of the island's central
peaks and valleys.

For lunch, try the small café at
Ribeiro Frio. If you prefer to bring
your own food, there are picnic
areas in the vicinity. Alternatively,
continue on to **Santana** *(see p81)*.

AFTERNOON

If you're not already in Santana,
make your way there to see the
traditional triangular houses and
the **Madeira Theme Park** *(see
p58)*. Next, follow signs to the
Rocha do Navio Teleférico, and
you will find a cable car and
footpath to **Santana's beach**.

Now head west into **Faial** *(see
p84)*. Two "balconies" along the
way give you memorable views
of **Penha de Águia** *(see p84)*.

If you're staying in Funchal, the
fastest route back is to follow
signs to Machico through a long
tunnel that links up with the
airport road back to the city.

See map on p80

The Best of the Rest

 São Roque de Faial
MAP J3

Several valleys meet at São Roque, so walkers can start at the church and choose one of the paths that go west up the Ribeiro Frio ("Cold River") or east up the Tem-te Não Caias (literally, "Hold On; Don't Fall").

 Boaventura
MAP G2

If you want to explore the orchards watered by the Levada de Cima, Boaventura makes a great base. Take a good walking guide with you.

São Jorge
MAP H2

A Baroque church from 1761 stands in São Jorge, and Ponta de São Jorge has a 19th-century lighthouse with coast views. A side road east of the village leads to a small, sheltered beach (see p53).

Eagle Rock or Penha de Águia

 Penha de Águia
MAP J3

"Eagle Rock" rises 590 m (1,935 ft) from the sea, casting its shadow over neighbouring villages. Young Madeirans regard the climb from Penha de Águia de Baixo to the top as a test of strength and endurance.

Queimadas
MAP H3

From western Santana, a road signposted to "Queimadas" gives way to a track leading to a house with gardens, ponds and picnic tables in the heart of the UNESCO World Natural Heritage forest.

 Ponta Delgada
MAP F2

At Ponta Delgada's church, see the miraculous statue found floating at sea in the 16th century. When the church burned down in 1908, it was found intact in the embers.

Faial
MAP J3

The Fortim do Faial is a toy-town fort built in the 18th century to fend off pirates. South of the village are views of Penha de Águia and an area where part of the cliff fell into the sea.

Lighthouse on Ponta de São Jorge

 Caldeirão Verde
MAP G3

From Queimadas, a scenic *levada* walk leads to the "Green Cauldron", a waterfall cascading down a rock hollow. Sturdy footwear, torches (flash-lights) and waterproofs are needed.

Terreiro da Luta
MAP H5

Pious Madeirans believe that the Virgin appeared to a young shepherd girl on this spot and gave her the statue now in Monte church. The memorial was erected after 1916.

Porto da Cruz
MAP J3

The Old Town is a maze of cobbled alleys. A sugar mill stands by the harbour, where visitors can buy the locally distilled spirit *aguardente*.

See map on p80

Places to Eat

1 **Adega da Quinta, Estreito de Câmara de Lobos**

MAP F5 ▪ Quinta do Estreito, Rua José Joaquim da Costa ▪ 291 910 530 ▪ €€€

Rustic Madeiran food is the speciality at this hotel restaurant. Sample the succulent *espetada* (meat kebab), roasted in a wood-burning oven.

2 **Quinta do Furão**

 MAP H2 ▪ Estrada Quinta do Furão 6 ▪ 291 570 100 ▪ €€

A combination of traditional Madeiran flavours and international influences is carefully prepared and presented. Great terrace views (see p61).

3 **São Cristóvão, Boaventura**

MAP F2 ▪ Sitio de São Cristóvão ▪ 291 863 031 ▪ €€

Along the northern central coast, this traditional Portufuese eatery has a good view of the sea and mountains.

4 **Vila do Peixe**

MAP F6 ▪ Rua Dr Joao Abel de Freitas, Câmara de Lobos ▪ 291 099 909 ▪ €€

A menu featuring the day's catch, simply prepared and served with a lovely harbour view (see p60).

5 **Churrascaria Caldeirão Verde, Santana**

MAP H2 ▪ Avenida Manuel Marques da Trindade ▪ 291 576 185 ▪ €

A great stand-by with no-frills service but excellent value grilled steak and skewered meats (espetada).

6 **Churrascaria O Lagar, Câmara de Lobos**

MAP F6 ▪ Estrada do João G Zarco 478 ▪ 291 941 865 ▪ €€€

A big palace in the hills serving tender garlic-flavoured chicken and skewers of beef, with warm *bolo de caco* bread.

7 **Sabores do Curral, Curral das Freiras**

MAP F4 ▪ Caminho da Igreja 1 ▪ 291 712 257 ▪ Closed Mon ▪ €€

This charming, rustic eatery offers traditional gastronomical delights of local produce with chestnut as the main ingredient. Try the liqueur.

8 **Vila da Carne**

MAP F6 ▪ Rua Dr. João Abel de Freitas, Câmara de Lobos ▪ 291 099 908 ▪ €€

Housed in the same space as Vila do Peixe, the restaurant is all about various meats. Sizzling *espetada* is the signature dish.

9 **Cantinho da Serra**

MAP H2 ▪ Estrada do Pico das Pedras 57, Santana ▪ 291 573 727 ▪ €

Hearty home cooking reinforces the warm, rustic ambience. In winter they heat the room with an inviting log fire (see p61)

10 **Casa Velha**

MAP H6 ▪ Casa Velha do Palheiro, Rua da Estalagem 23, São Gonçalo ▪ 291 790 350 ▪ €€€

A stately charm pervades this country style dining room, all Villeroy & Boch tableware and floral trim. Expect haute cuisine and fine wines.

Casa Velha do Palheiro

🔟 Western Madeira

The Valley Road linking Ribeira Brava and São Vicente via the Encumeada Pass forms the boundary between the high peaks of central Madeira and the flat moorland of the Paúl da Serra plateau to the west. Ridges and ravines run down the plateau escarpment. Those to the north plunge almost sheer to the sea, with waterfalls that cascade for hundreds of feet. Farming villages cling to the gentler slopes to the south and west, where new roads are opening up beautiful unexplored areas.

Panoramic view of the dramatic cliffs at the bay of Seixal

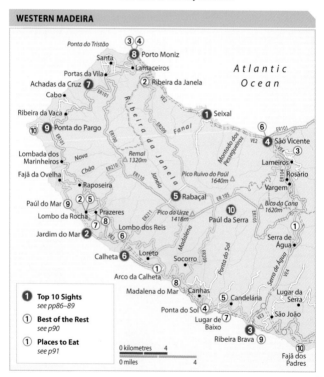

WESTERN MADEIRA

Ponta do Tristão

③ ④
⑧ Porto Moniz

Santa
• Lamaceiros

Portas da Vila •
② Ribeira da Janela

Achadas da Cruz ⑦
ER101

Cabo •

A t l a n t i c
O c e a n

Ribeira da Vaca •

① Seixal

⑩ ⑨ Ponta do Pargo
ER101

⑥ ER101
VE2 ④ São Vicente
③

Lombada dos Marinheiros
Nova
Remal △ 1320m

Lameiros

Fajã da Ovelha
Chão ER210
ER110
Pico Ruivo do Paúl 1640m △
Rosário
Vargem

• Raposeira
⑤ Rabaçal ER105
Bica da Cana 1620m

Paúl do Mar ⑨ ② ⑤
ER211 Pico da Urze △ 1418m
⑩ Paúl da Serra
①

Lombo da Rocha ⑦ ⑧ • Prazeres
Lombo dos Reis
Serra de Água •

Jardim do Mar ② ⑥
VE3
Madalena

Serra de Água

Calheta ⑥ • Loreto
Socorro

Arco da Calheta ①

Madalena do Mar ⑧ Canhas
⑤ Candelária
Lugar da Serra

Ponta do Sol ④
⑦ São João

Lugar de Baixo
VE3

③
Ribeira Brava ⑨

Top 10 Sights
see pp86–89

① **Best of the Rest**
see p90

① **Places to Eat**
see p91

⑩ Fajã dos Padres

0 kilometres   4

0 miles   4

1 Seixal

MAP D2 ■ Rodoeste buses 80 and 139

Most of the coastal road now runs through tunnels, but from Seixal you can get a sense of the north coast's visual splendour. Tall cliffs stretching into the distance are pounded by powerful waves. Vineyards cling to the rock on almost vertical terraces. Waterfalls plunge from the wooded heights on either side of the village.

2 Jardim do Mar

MAP B4 ■ Rodoeste buses 80 and 163

This pretty village (literally, "Garden of the Sea") sits at the meeting-point of ancient cobbled footpaths, which climb up the cliffs. In the village, a maze of alleys winds down to a pebble beach, where surfing competitions are held during the winter. A large sea-wall makes surfing here tricky, even for the very experienced.

3 Ribeira Brava

MAP D5 ■ Rodoeste buses 4, 6, 7, 80, 127, 139 and 142 ■ Museu Etnográfico da Madeira: Rua São Francisco 24; 291 952 598; open 9:30am–5pm Tue–Fri, 10am–12:30pm & 1:30–5:30pm Sat–Sun; adm

Ribeira Brava (literally, "Wild Stream") is one of the island's oldest towns, well established as a centre of sugar production by the 1440s. The parish church has sculpture from the 1480s. The Museu Etnográfico da Madeira is worth a visit; it also has a crafts shop.

Historical centre of São Vicente

4 São Vicente

MAP E2 ■ Rodoeste buses 6 and 139

This pretty village on the northern side of the Encumeada Pass would be wonderful to paint: deep-green shutters, doors and balconies, with stone lintels and frames of ox-blood red, are set in white-walled houses along the grey basalt streets.

5 Rabaçal

MAP C3

Washed by centuries of rain running from the flat surface of the Paúl da Serra, Rabaçal is a green cleft in the moorland. A brisk 2-km (1-mile) walk down a winding tarmac path goes through heather to a forest house with picnic tables. Rabaçal marks the start of two popular signposted walks. One follows the Levada do Risco to the Risco Waterfall (30 minutes there and back); the other leads down to 25 Fontes ("25 Springs"), a cauldron-like pool fed by many falls (1 hour 40 minutes there and back).

Large parish church of Ribeira Brava

⑥ Calheta

MAP B4 ▪ Rodoeste buses 80, 142, 163 and 164 ▪ Calheta Church: open 10am–1pm & 4–6pm daily ▪ Engenho da Calheta: 291 822 264; open 8am–7pm Tue–Sun

Standing on a terrace halfway up the hill leading west out of the village, Calheta's fine parish church is a scaled-down version of Funchal cathedral *(see pp12–13)*. The church contains a precious 17th-century ebony-and-silver tabernacle, and a richly decorated *alfarge* (knotwork) ceiling above the high altar. Next door to the church is the Engenho da Calheta, one of Madeira's two surviving sugar mills; the other is in Porto da Cruz *(see p84)*. As well as producing *mel* (honey), which is used in making the island's unique *bolo de mel* (honey cake), the mill also manufactures *aguardente* (rum) using distilled cane syrup.

Fields of Achadas da Cruz

⑦ Achadas da Cruz

MAP B2 ▪ Cable car: Caminho do Teleférico, Achadas da Cruz ▪ 291 852 951 ▪ 8am–noon, 1–6pm daily ▪ adm

Little visited, perhaps due to a lack of signage, this corner of the island is worth making the effort to explore. The village is nondescript except for the fact that it is the departure point for one of the most memorable and knee-trembling cable car rides in Madeira. The gondola glides over the edge of a 450-m (1,476-ft) cliff to take you down to a rocky beach and a few huts below via a jaw-dropping view.

Rough seas and rocks at Porto Moniz

⑧ Porto Moniz

MAP C1 ▪ Rodoeste buses 80 and 139

At the most northwesterly point on the island is Porto Moniz, which comprises a bustling agricultural town set high up around its church, with a lower town devoted to food and bathing. Natural rock pools have been turned into a bathing complex offering a safe environment in which to enjoy the exhilarating experience of being showered by spray from waves breaking on the offshore rocks. The landscaped seafront is lined with restaurants selling some of the island's best seafood.

⑨ Ponta do Pargo

MAP A2 ▪ Rodoeste buses 80 and 142

Madeira's westernmost point, Ponta do Pargo is the best place on the island to watch the setting sun or to gaze down at the waves breaking along the tall cliffs of the island's coasts. The lighthouse set on the headland dates from the early 20th century and has a small exhibition of maps and photographs charting the history of lighthouses on every island in the Madeiran archipelago. The ceiling of the parish church depicts colourful sunsets, terraced hills, and the scenic spots of the western part of the island. They were all painted in the 1990s by a Belgian artist who settled in the village.

Paúl da Serra
MAP D3

The undulating plateau of Paúl da Serra ("Mountain Marsh") is where the waters that feed many of the island's streams and *levadas* gather. It acts as a sponge for the abundant rains that fall when clouds reach the island, rise, then cool. Free-range horned cattle graze the lush grass. People from the nearby villages pick wild bilberries and blackberries in summer, which they turn into tasty conserves. Many also depend on the plateau's wind turbines for electricity.

SUGAR REVIVAL

The sugar mills at Calheta and Porto da Cruz date from the sugar renaissance of the 19th century, when the demand for high-quality sugar increased dramatically, thanks to the popularity of sweetmeats in genteel European households. The nuns of Santa Clara (*see p20*) were especially renowned for their preserves, marzipan sweets, crystallized figs and other delights.

A DAY IN WESTERN MADEIRA

▶ MORNING

The first stop on this long but rewarding trip is **Ribeira Brava** (*see p87*), located 25 minutes from Funchal by the winding south coast highway. If you arrive before the Museu Etnográfico da Madeira opens, enjoy a coffee on the seafront or take a look inside the **São Bento** church (*see p47*). Driving north on the ER104 (VE4), follow signs to Serra de Água. For spectacular mountain views, avoid the highway tunnel route to **São Vicente** (*see p87*). Turn off along the way for refreshments at **Pousada dos Vinháticos** (*see p91*) and absorb those jaw-dropping vistas. Descending to São Vicente, spare some time for a short but fascinating tour of the **Grutas de São Vicente** (*see p58*). For a good lunch head to the seafront and **O Cachalote** (*see p91*).

AFTERNOON

Porto Moniz can be reached via the modern highway, with the old ER101 (*Antiga*) coastal road deemed too dangerous due to rock falls. If it's hot, take a dip in the natural **rock pools** (*see p53*). Otherwise, take the ER110 for a pleasant undulating drive across the **Paúl da Serra** plateau. Pause at **Rabaçal** (*see p87*) and stretch your legs along the *levada* path that leads to a waterfall (*see p55*). Allow at least an hour to explore this woodland world. Head back via the Encumeada Pass to rejoin the ER104 (VE4) back to Funchal.

See map on p86 ←

The Best of the Rest

 Arco da Calheta
MAP C4

An early church survives at the heart of this sprawling village. The Capela do Loreto, founded by the wife of Zarco's grandson, dates from the mid-15th-century.

 Ribeira da Janela
MAP C1

This wild, uninhabited valley joins the sea beside a rocky islet with a hole like a window (its name is "Window Valley"). The road descends through a misty world of ancient trees kept moist by the condensation of clouds.

Ribeira da Janela road

3 Lime Route Museum Centre
MAP E3 ■ Sítio da Achada do Furtado do Barrinho, Lameiros ■ 291 842 018 ■ 10am–5pm Tue–Sat ■ sites.google.com/site/rotadacal/

There are two lime quarries, a kiln, haylofts and a *levada*, all preserved at this engaging cultural and heritage museum centre.

4 Ponta do Sol
MAP D5 ■ Rua Príncipe Dom Luís 3 ■ 291 974 034

The American novelist John dos Passos (1896–1970) visited this village in 1960 to see the home of his grandparents. The house has since been turned into a cultural centre.

5 Lombada
MAP D5

On a ridge above Ponta do Sol is one of Madeira's oldest houses – the 15th-century mansion of Columbus's friend João Esmeraldo *(see p74)*. The watermill opposite is fed by one of the island's oldest *levadas*. A pretty church of 1722 is lined with tile pictures of the Virtues.

6 Lombo dos Reis
MAP B4

The "Ridge of the Kings" is named after the tiny, rustic Capela dos Reis Magos ("Chapel of the Three Kings"), with a 16th-century Flemish altar carving of the Nativity.

7 Lugar de Baixo
MAP D5

Above the tiny freshwater lagoon at Lugar de Baixo is a visitor centre with pictures of the wild birds that frequent this shore, though you will mostly see domesticated ducks and moorhens.

8 Prazeres
MAP B3

The priest at Prazeres has set up a small children's farm opposite the church. The main attraction is the flower-lined path along the Levada Nova (New Levada).

9 Paúl do Mar
MAP A3

The best approach to this fishing (and surfing) village is down the twisting road from Fajã de Orvela. On the way, look out for a glimpse of the stunning Galinas Gorge.

10 Fajã dos Padres
MAP E5 ■ Estrada Padre António Dinis Henriques 1, Fajã dos Padres ■ 291 944 538 ■ www.fajadospadres.com

A cable car carries visitors down to a restaurant on a pebble beach fronting vineyards and vegetable gardens.

See map on p86

Places to Eat

PRICE CATEGORIES
For a three course meal for one with half
a bottle of wine (or equivalent meal),
taxes and extra charges.

€ under €25 €€ €25–€60 €€€ over €60

**1 Pousada dos Vinháticos,
Serra de Água**
MAP E4 ■ 291 952 344 ■ €€€

The food is perfectly good but it is
upstaged by views looking out onto
Madeira's most Wagnerian mountain
landscapes, lit by the setting sun.

**2 Jardim Atlântico,
Prazeres**
MAP B3 ■ Lombo da Rocha ■ 291 820
220 ■ €€

The best bet for vegetarians looking
for an escape from an endless diet
of omelettes, the restaurant at the
Jardim Atlântico Hotel sources its
produce from local market gardens.

**3 O Cachalote, Porto
Moniz**
MAP C1 ■ Praia do Porto Moniz ■ 291
853 180 ■ Closed D daily ■ €€€

Long regarded as the best seafood
restaurant in Porto Moniz, O Cachalote
now has competition from several
other places in this popular resort.

4 Orca, Porto Moniz
MAP C1 ■ Rotunda das
Piscinas ■ 291 850 000 ■ €

There's a selection of well-
presented cheese boards and
tapas plus a surprisingly eclectic
wine list at this café-shop, which
also sells souvenirs.

**5 Solar dos Prazeres,
Prazeres**
MAP B3 ■ Lombo da Rocha
■ 291 822 759 ■ €€

Enjoy splendid ocean and
mountain views while
savouring grilled cod and
espetada de carne (grilled
meat kebab) at this extremely
popular eatery.

6 Quebramar
MAP E2 ■ Sítio do Calhau, São
Vicente ■ 291 842 338 ■ €

Tuna steaks and tender medallions
of pork are just two of the dishes
enlightening the menu at this bright
and breezy seafront eatery.

**7 O Manjerico, Arco da
Calheta**
MAP B3 ■ Caminho da Referta, Pico
Prazeres ■ 291 822 897 ■ €

Renowned for its stuffed chicken,
this homely eatery is a little off the
beaten track but worth the diversion.
Call ahead for reservations.

8 Cantinho da Madalena
MAP C4 ■ Avenida 1 de
Fevereio 2, Madalena do Mar ■ 291
972 235 ■ €€€

Grab a seat on the terrace and
enjoy a typical Madeiran meal
at this local favourite.

**9 Borda D´Água, Ribeira
Brava**
MAP D5 ■ Rua Engenheiro Ribeiro
Pereira ■ 291 957 697 ■ Dis access
■ €€

Wholesome fresh fish and seafood
characterizes the menu at this popular oceanfront venue. Vegetarian
options are available.

**10 Casa de Chá "O Fío",
Ponta do Pargo**
MAP A2 ■ Sitio do Salão de Baixo
■ 291 882 525 ■ €€

A teahouse isn't what you'd expect
to find on a clifftop, but
many come here for
homemade soups
and light meals.

Casa de Chá

TOP 10 Eastern Madeira

Most visitors catch a glimpse of Eastern Madeira as they fly in over Machico, the island's second biggest town, and travel from the airport to Funchal along the south coast highway. However, there are wide expanses where no roads go. These include the north coast, with its paths and vertigo-inducing cliffs, and the historic whaling village of Caniçal, the charming town of Santa Cruz and the pastoral landscape of the Santo da Serra plateau, source of the island's wicker.

Steep cliffs of Ponta São Lourenço

1 Ponta de São Lourenço
MAP M4

The long, narrow chain of eroded volcanic cliffs and ravines at the eastern tip of Madeira is an exciting and dramatic wilderness, protected as a nature reserve because of its coastal plants. The rocky peninsula can be explored by the much-used path that starts from the car park at the end of the south coast road.

EASTERN MADEIRA

0 km   2
0 miles   2

Ilhas Selvagens
285 km (176 miles)

Ilhas Desertas

0 km   15
0 miles   15

Previous pages: Traditional A-frame house, Santana district

② The Ilhas Desertas
MAP J1

Ponta de São Lourenço is linked underwater to the offshore Ilhas Desertas (meaning "Deserted Islands"), which are part of the same volcanic formation. Though arid and uninhabited, these islands nevertheless host all sorts of rare and endangered wildlife, including spiders, monk seals, petrels and shearwaters. For a closer look, contact one of the boat companies based at Funchal marina, many of which offer day-long trips to the islands *(see p57)*.

③ Santa Cruz
MAP K5 ▪ SAM bus 20, 23, 53, 60, 78, 113,156

A town of great character, Santa Cruz is surprisingly peaceful, considering that the airport runway is situated right next door. The focal points are the beach and the seafront, which is lined with cafés and *pastelarias* (pastry shops), as well as the Art Deco-style Palm Beach Lido, painted azure and cream. Set back from the coast, past winding alleys, stands a 15th-century Gothic church, which is as splendid as the cathedral in Funchal, and perhaps designed by the same architect *(see p12)*.

Fortress on the seafront at Machico

④ Machico
MAP K4 ▪ SAM bus 20, 23, 53, 78, 113,156

This is where Captain Zarco and his crew landed on Madeira in 1420. The chapel they founded *(see p47)* is on the eastern side of the harbour. A statue of Machico's first governor, Tristão Vaz Teixeira, stands in front of the main square's 15th-century church. Cobbled alleys lead from here to the seafront. The Solar do Ribeirinho Museum, in a 17th-century manor house, is worth a visit.

Sunbathing on the beach in the pleasant town of Santa Cruz

5 Garajau
MAP J6

A miniature version of Rio de Janeiro's statue of Christ the Redeemer was erected on the wild and rocky headland at the southern end of the village in 1927. The terns (garajau in Portuguese) that gave their name to the village can still be seen from the zigzag path that winds down the cliff face to a pebble beach below the headland. Underwater caves and reefs rich in marine life extend for 2 km (1 mile) to either side, and form a marine reserve (see p98).

6 Portela
MAP J4 ■ SAM bus 20, 53, 78

The viewing point at Portela has more than its fair share of roadside cafés because it was once the transport hub for the east of the island. Tunnels linking São Roque do Faial with Machico have changed all that, but Portela is still an important landmark for walkers. You can walk south from here to Porto da Cruz (see p84) along a trail once used by wine carriers, or west along the Levada do Portela through dense primeval woodland and mountain scenery to Ribeiro Frio (see p83).

Porta da Cruz seen from Portela

Statue of Christ the Redeemer, Garajau

7 Santo António da Serra
MAP J4 ■ Carros de São Gonçalo bus 77; SAM bus 20, 25, 78

The village of Santo António da Serra (known to Madeirans simply as Santo da Serra), sits in the middle of a plateau flat enough for golf courses (see p57) and fields of grazing cows. Despite its frequent cloud cover, wealthy English merchants once built rural homes here: one of the former homes of the Blandy family (see p17) is now a public park with camellias, hydrangeas, rhododendrons, deer and horse enclosures, and viewing points that look out toward Ponta de São Lourenço.

8 Caniço de Baixo
MAP J6 ■ Galomar Lido: open summer 9am–7pm, winter 10am–5pm; adm

Before heading to this charming clifftop holiday village, stop to admire fine Baroque decoration at Caniço's 18th-century Igreja Matriz in Rua Jão Paulo II. The tiny Praia da Canavieira public beach is reached down an easily missed alley near the junction with Rua da Falésia. For a small sum, you can also use the Galomar Lido. The lido is the base for the Manta Diving Centre, which organizes trips to the Garajau Marine Reserve.

9 Caniçal
MAP L4 ▪ SAM bus 113

A former whaling port, Caniçal is where director John Huston came to shoot the opening scenes of *Moby Dick* in 1956. Unfortunately, its star Gregory Peck became seasick and they had to shoot the rest of the movie in a studio. The Museu da Baleia *(see p49)* uses 3D and interactive displays to explain how conservation has replaced whaling.

Wickerwork demonstration, Camacha

10 Camacha
MAP J5 ▪ Carros de São Gonçalo bus 77, 110, 129; Horários do Funchal bus 113

A monument in the centre of Camacha declares that Portugal's first ever game of football was played here in 1875. However, it is the O Relógio ("The Clock") wicker factory *(see p66)* that draws people here. You can see demonstrations of wicker-making in the workshop. In the back streets of the village, you can spot stacks of freshly cut willow canes. These are steeped in water and stripped of bark, then boiled to make them pliable.

THE ILHAS SELVAGENS

Also part of the Madeiran archipelago are the arid, treeless Ilhas Selvagens ("Wild Islands"), which lie 285 km (178 miles) south of Madeira and 165 km (103 miles) north of Tenerife, in the Canaries. These volcanic islets, claimed by Portugal in 1458, have Europe's largest nesting colonies of rare storm petrels and shearwaters. Military sentries from the Nature Guards are stationed on the islands to protect the birds.

A DAY IN EASTERN MADEIRA

▶ MORNING

After breakfast in Funchal, take the south coast highway by following signs to the airport, then take the São Gonçalo exit and head for **Camacha**. The road passes the **Quinta do Palheiro Ferreiro** gardens *(see pp32–3)*. Camacha is famous for its wicker, so browse **O Relógio** *(see p66)* on the main square for an exhibition of wickerwork. Carry on to **Santo António da Serra** for a walk in the wooded park. Then continue through the village and turn left where the road forks for **Machico** *(see p95)*, known for the **Capela dos Milagres** *(see p47)* and sandy Banda d'Além beach *(see p52)*. After exploring the town, head for lunch at **Maré Alta** *(see p99)*.

AFTERNOON

The onward drive to **Caniçal** is rewarded with an excellent visitor attraction, the **Museu da Baleia** *(see p49)*. If it's hot and sunny there's also the attractive beach at nearby **Prainha** *(see p52)* to relax on. A little further on is Baia D'Abra, the starting point for one of the most exhilarating coastal hikes in Madeira – the **Ponta de Sao Lourenço** trail *(see p54)*. Depending on your schedule, you can elect to walk the entire route to Morro do Furado and back, an 8-km (5-mile) ramble of around four hours' duration. Alternatively, try the shorter path to Seahorse Rocks for picture-postcard views and return within the hour. Head back toward Funchal and leave the south coast highway at **Santa Cruz** *(see p95)* for refreshments.

See map on p94 ←

Garajau Marine Reserve Sights

Male Mediterranean monk seal

mammals are seen all over the reserve. Social and playful, they are best observed as part of an organized ocean excursion *(see p57)*.

6 Atlantic Manta Ray

Diving face to face with these majestic fish as they glide gracefully is a real treat. Effortlessly fanning the water, their triangular pectoral fins can span up to 7 m (23 ft) in width.

1 Mediterranean Monk Seal

One of Europe's most endangered mammals, the monk seal is an increasingly frequent visitor to the reserve. Slender, agile and shy, they are more likely to be seen on day trips to the Ilhas Desertas *(see p95)* where a colony of around 30 thrive.

2 Dusky Grouper

The rocky seabed is an ideal habitat for these large, friendly fish. Naturally curious, they'll often swim just an arm's length away from divers.

3 Sperm Whale

A permanent resident of the waters around Madeira, this is the whale species you are most likely to encounter on whale-watching trips *(see p58)*. The best time to see them is from March to September.

4 Trumpetfish

Often seen swimming upright, blending in with vertical coral, these pencil-like fish vary from brown to greenish or yellow. They are very well camouflaged and hard to spot.

5 Bottlenose Dolphin

Year-round residents but here in greater numbers from March to October, pods of these intelligent

7 Loggerhead Turtle

With its slow, deliberate paddle, this gentle and endearing creature always appears as if it hasn't a care in the world. Often seen near the water's surface, loggerheads are considered an endangered species and the reserve provides a welcome sanctuary.

8 Mediterranean Parrotfish

This eccentrically coloured fish can brighten up even the dullest day. Distinguished by its vivid scarlet patch coat replete with yellow trim and silver-blue bands, it is a wonderfully photogenic species.

9 Zino's Petrel

Endemic to Madeira, this is one of the most endangered seabirds of Europe. Elegant in flight, it is seen out at sea during the day; it comes inshore only at night to nest in the high mountainous interior.

10 Great Shearwater

One of six species of shearwater that can be observed off the Madeiran coast, the great shearwater is sighted occasionally in the strait between the island and the Ilhas Desertas, gliding just above the waves, scarcely moving its wings.

→ *See map on p94*

Places to Eat

1 Abrigo do Pastor, Camacha

MAP J5 ▪ Estrada das Carreiras 209 ▪ 291 922 060 ▪ Closed Tue ▪ €€

Enjoy hearty, homemade country fare at this rustic eatery. Leave room for afters, with pumpkin cheesecake a favourite dessert *(see p61)*.

2 Muralha's Bar, Caniçal

MAP L4 ▪ Rua da Pedra d'Eira ▪ 291 961 468 ▪ €

The simple vibe here belies some truly delicious food. Try a plate of *lapas* (grilled limpets drizzled with lemon juice) and a cold beer. Not far from the Museu da Baleia *(see p49)*.

3 Atlantis, Caniço de Baixo

MAP J6 ▪ Ponta D'Oliveira ▪ 291 930 930 ▪ €

The restaurant appears hewn out of the cliff, and you dine to the sound of the ocean thundering onto the beach. The seafood excels, as do the views.

4 A Casa dos Cavalos, Santo da Serra

MAP J4 ▪ Sítio da Lagoa ▪ 291 552 259 ▪ €€

With an equestrian theme, the menu at this rural eatery is surprisingly eclectic, with tapas and other Mediterranean dishes listed.

5 Avó Micas, Santo da Serra

MAP J4 ▪ Porto Bay Serra Golf Hotel, Sítio dos Casais Próximos ▪ 291 550 500 ▪ €€€

Traditional Madeiran dishes, such as pork marinated in wine and garlic, are served at this eatery.

6 Bar Amarelo, Caniçal

MAP L4 ▪ Caniçal ▪ 291 961 798 ▪ €€

This harbourside gem has a decor of limestone and steel that stands out. Choose from salads, pasta or grilled fish.

PRICE CATEGORIES

For a three course meal for one with half a bottle of wine (or equivalent meal), taxes and extra charges.

€ under €25   €€ €25–€60   €€€ over €60

7 Mercado Velho, Machico

MAP K4 ▪ Rua do Mercado ▪ 291 965 926 ▪ €€

The courtyard of the old seafront market in Machico has been turned into an alfresco restaurant serving grilled fish and meat.

8 Café Relógio, Camacha

MAP J5 ▪ Largo Conselheiro Aires de Ornelas 12 ▪ 291 922 777 ▪ €€

Come here on Saturday to see one of Madeira's top folk song-and-dance acts. Local dishes here as well as specials, such as smoked fish, and grilled prawns in chilli and garlic.

9 Maré Alta, Machico

MAP K4 ▪ Largo da Praça ▪ 291 607 126 ▪ €

The windows afford broad harbour views, and the food is of the ocean, super fresh and served promptly. If there's a table, opt for the terrace.

10 La Perla, Caniço de Baixo

MAP J6 ▪ Quinta Splendida Hotel, Estrada da Ponta Oliveira 11 ▪ 291 930 400 ▪ Open Wed–Sun ▪ €€€

Seafood *risotto au champagne* and veal with rosemary exemplify the international menu *(see p60)*.

La Perla at Caniço de Baixo

TOP 10 Porto Santo

Porto Santo lies 43 km (27 miles) northeast of Madeira. Zarco and his crew stopped here in 1418 on their way to explore Africa's west coast. Realizing that the island would be a good base, he returned in 1419 to plant the Portuguese flag, going on to Madeira the next year. Early settlers introduced rabbits and goats, which quickly stripped the island of its vegetation, so Porto Santo is not green like Madeira. Instead, the "Golden Island" has a magnificent sandy beach and attracts holidaymakers with its sunshine, sea and agreeable sense of being a very long way from the busy world.

Beautiful golden sands of Porto Santo's wide beach

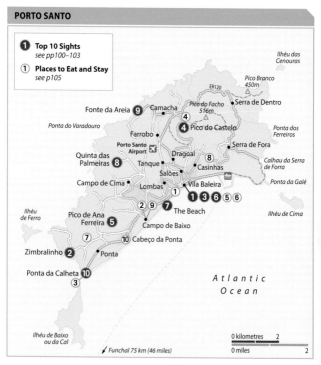

PORTO SANTO

1 Top 10 Sights
see pp100–103

① Places to Eat and Stay
see p105

Ilhéu das Cenouras

Pico Branco 450m

ER120

Serra de Dentro

Fonte da Areia **9**   Camacha   Pico do Facho 516m   **4**

4 Pico do Castelo

Ponta do Varadouro

Farrobo •

Ponta dos Ferreiros

Porto Santo Airport

Serra de Fora

Quinta das Palmeiras **8**   Tanque •   Dragoal •   **8**   Casinhas •

Calhau da Serra de Forra

Campo de Cima •   Salões •

Lombas •   **• Vila Baleira**

Ponta da Galé

Ilhéu de Ferro

1 3 6 5 6

2 9 7   The Beach

Ilhéu de Cima

Pico de Ana Ferreira **5**

Campo de Baixo

7   **10** Cabeço da Ponta

Zimbralinho **2**   • Ponta

Ponta da Calheta **10**

3

Atlantic Ocean

Ilhéu de Baixo ou da Cal

✈ *Funchal 75 km (46 miles)*

0 kilometres   2

0 miles   2

1 Vila Baleira
MAP L2

All life on the island centres on this city, which sits roughly halfway along the southern coast. Pavement cafés fill the main square, Largo do Pelourinho ("Pillory Square"), where offenders were once punished and public proclamations read out. The town hall, with its double staircase flanked by dragon trees, stands on the site of the pillory. The cobbled pavement in front has a glass-topped, stone-lined pit, which was once used for storing grain.

Nossa Senhora da Piedade

2 Zimbralinho
MAP K2

Boasting transparent blue seas popular with swimmers and divers, Zimbralinho is the most beautiful of all the little rocky coves nestling along the western flank of the island. The cove is at its best around lunchtime, as it is shaded earlier and later in the day. The path to the cove starts at the end of the road that leads to the Centro Hípico (see p104), at the western end of the island.

3 Nossa Senhora da Piedade
MAP L2

To the east of the main square in Vila Baleira stands the majestic parish church, Nossa Senhora da Piedade, completed in 1446. Gothic rib-vaulting and rainwater spouts carved with human and animal heads have

survived from this earlier church, which was torched by pirates, then rebuilt in 1667. The 17th-century altar painting of Christ being laid in his tomb is by Portuguese artist Martím Conrado. The saints on either side were painted in 1945 by German artist Max Römer (see p16).

4 Pico do Castelo
MAP L1

East of Vila Baleira is Castle Peak, though – despite its name – it was never actually fortified. From the 15th century on, it was used as a place of refuge whenever pirates threatened to attack. It was equipped with a cannon, which survives at the lookout point near the summit. A cobbled road leads to the lookout, past the cypress, cedar and pine trees planted to turn the slopes from sandy to green.

Green slopes of Pico do Castelo

Organ pipe rock columns at Pico de Ana Ferreira

5 Pico de Ana Ferreira
MAP K2

Porto Santo consists of a saddle of land between two groups of cone-shaped volcanic peaks. At 283 m (929 ft), Pico de Ana Ferreira is the highest of the summits at the more developed western end of the island. A road up its southern slopes will take you as far as the 17th-century Church of São Pedro. From there, a track leads around the peak to a disused quarry with an interesting formation of prismatic basalt columns known as the "Organ Pipes".

6 Casa Museu Cristóvão Colombo
MAP L2 ▪ Travessa da Sacristia 2–4 ▪ 291 983 405 ▪ Open 10am–12:30pm & 2–5:30pm Tue–Sat (until 7pm Jul, Aug & Sep), 10am–1pm Sun ▪ Adm ▪ www.museucolombo-portosanto.com

Christopher Columbus (1451–1506) came to Madeira in 1478 as the agent for a Lisbon sugar merchant.

Christopher Columbus's house

He married Filipa Moniz, daughter of the governor of Porto Santo, but she died soon after their son was born in 1479 and Columbus left the islands in 1480. The house where they are said to have lived is now a museum, with portraits of Columbus, maps of his voyages and models of his ships.

7 The Beach
MAP L2

Millions of years ago, sandstone, limestone and coral were laid down on top of Porto Santo's volcanic rocks beneath a warm, shallow sea. Falling sea levels exposed the coral to erosion, and the result is the 10-km (6-mile) sweep of sand that runs along the southern side of the island. Backed by dunes and tamarisk trees, the sand is divided into several areas, of which Fontinha and Ribeiro Salgado have been awarded Blue Flag status for environmental quality. Burying yourself in the sand is said to bring relief from rheumatism and arthritis.

8 Quinta das Palmeiras
MAP L2 ▪ Estrada das Pedras Vermelhas, Sítio dos Linhares ▪ 291 983 625 ▪ 10am–1pm & 3–5pm daily ▪ Adm

Located in the western part of the island, this little botanical garden and zoo sits a bit incongruously in the arid landscape. It offers plenty of welcome shade for the collection of subtropical flora and exotic birdlife that includes parrots, waterfowl and a pair of emus. The landscaped pond is home to plump golden carp. As much a working farm as a visitor attraction, the *quinta* is ideal for a family visit, with a play area cordoned off for kids. There is also a well-stocked café in which to unwind.

⑨ Fonte da Areia
MAP L1

Water once bubbled straight out of the sandstone cliffs at Fonte da Areia ("Fountain of Sand"), but in 1843 the spring was tamed, and visitors can now taste the natural, rock-filtered mineral water by turning a tap. The path to the spring leads down a wind-eroded gully, where the cliffs have been sculpted into laminated sheets of harder and softer rock.

WATER, WINE AND LIME

Water, wine and lime were once Porto Santo's economic staples. Mineral water was bottled opposite the Torre Praia Hotel access road. Quicklime (used in mortar) made in lime kilns like the one at the Torre Praia was exported. You can still buy Listrão Branco, the local fortified wine, but less is made every year.

---

⑩ Ponta da Calheta
MAP K2

The westernmost tip of the island is a beautiful spot, with a series of secluded sandy coves reached by scrambling over rocks. From the bar and restaurant at the end of the coast road, you can look across to Ilhéu de Baixo, the large, uninhabited rocky islet southwest of Porto Santo. Madeira, too, is visible on the distant horizon, usually capped by clouds.

Rocky shore at Ponta da Calheta

A DAY ON PORTO SANTO

 MORNING

Hire a car or scooter *(see p104)* for this tour, though you could do it by taxi. Drive northeast out of **Vila Baleira** *(see p101)*, up to the viewing point at **Portela** *(see p96)*. You will see three windmills of a type once common here. Carry on around the eastern end of the island, until a turning to the right takes you down to Serra de Fora beach. Some 2 km (1 mile) further north are traditional stone houses at Serra de Dentro and fine views from Pico Branco. From the Camacha crossroads, a drivable track to the left leads up **Pico do Castelo** *(see p101)*, soon turning into a stone-paved road. The viewing point at the top has great views over central Porto Santo. Back at Camacha, there are several cafés for lunch.

AFTERNOON

First stop after lunch is **Fonte da Areia**. Despite looking arid, Porto Santo has several natural springs like this one. Then head to **Quinta das Palmeiras** to enjoy the sub-tropical gardens and exotic birds. Next, drive towards Campo de Cima. Alongside the airport runway, you will see some of the vineyards that still produce wine. Take the road up **Pico de Ana Ferreira**, then continue on foot to see its extraordinary-looking basalt columns. Afterwards, drive on to the stunning western tip of Porto Santo, **Ponta da Calheta**. You should have plenty of time for a drink at the "Sunset Bar" *(see p105)* on the beach, relaxing on the sand, or a swim before you head back to Vila Baleira.

See map on p100 ←

Activities

1 Sightseeing
MAP L2

Two-hour tours in open-topped buses depart daily at 2pm from the bus stop by the petrol station on the eastern side of the jetty.

Porto Santo sightseeing bus

2 Exploring by Car
Moinho Rent-a-Car: MAP L2; 291 982 141

Taxis offer island tours, but to explore independently, you can hire a car from Moinho Rent-a-Car.

3 Exploring by Bike
Auto Acessórios Colombo: MAP L2; 291 984 438 ▪ Porto Santo Line: MAP L2; 291 210 300

Auto Acessórios Colombo (opposite the road to the Torre Praia Hotel) rents out bicycles, scooters and quad bikes. Bikes can be hired in advance from Porto Santo Line. Collect a bike when you arrive at Porto Santo quay, and return it before the voyage back.

4 Walking
MAP M1

The trail that leads to the top of Pico Branco, Porto Santo's second-highest peak, offers fine views across the island from the Terra Chã lookout.

5 Watersports
Mar Dourado: MAP L2; 963 970 789

Mar Dourado, at Praia da Fontinha beach below the Torre Praia Hotel, rents out pedalos and kayaks, and will organize paragliding, water skiing, windsurfing and boat trips.

6 Tennis
Porto Santo Tennis Academy: MAP L2; Campo de Baixo; 291 983 274

The Porto Santo Tennis Academy, set next to the golf course, is fully equipped to competition standard. The main stadium has six courts.

7 Diving
Porto Santo Sub: MAP L2; Marina; 916 033 997 ▪ Rhea Dive: MAP L2; Rua Dr José Diamantino Lima; 964 500 557

Thanks to the unpolluted seas and the absence of commercial fishing, Porto Santo's shores are rich in marine life. Try either Porto Santo Sub or Rhea Dive for diving trips.

8 Horse Riding
Hipicenter: MAP K2; Sítio da Ponta; 291 983 258

Porto Santo's Hipicenter (equestrian centre) will take both children and adults at all skill levels.

9 Shopping
Centro do Artesanato: MAP L2; next to the quay

Shells, model ships and other souvenirs with a nautical theme are the stock-in-trade of Porto Santo's craft shops, which you will find located in the Centro do Artesanato.

10 Golf
Porto Santo Golfe: MAP L2; Sítio das Marinhas; 291 983 778

Designed by Severiano Ballesteros, Porto Santo Golfe has an 18-hole, par 72 course and a 9-hole, par 3 pitch-and-putt course.

The Porto Santo golf course

Places to Eat

PRICE CATEGORIES

For a three course meal for one with half a bottle of wine (or equivalent meal), taxes and extra charges.

€ under €25 €€ €25–60 €€€ over €60

Pé na Água, Vila Baleira
MAP L2 ▪ Sitio das Pedras Pretas (beyond the Torre Praia Hotel) ▪ 291 985 242 ▪ €€€

Not quite "foot in water" as the name suggests, but you are right by the sand at this boardwalk spot. The chef cooks a great seafood rice, as well as grilled fish and beef kebabs.

2 Vila Alencastre, Porto Santo
MAP L2 ▪ Estrada do Forno do Cal, Campo de Baixo ▪ 291 985 072 ▪ €€€

Filete de peixe-espada com banana (swordfish fillet with banana) and *arroz de pato* (duck rice) are specialities at this rustic eatery.

3 Ponta da Calheta, Calheta
MAP K2 ▪ 291 985 322 ▪ €€€

The "Sunset Bar" has an enviable position at the western end of the island, where you can sip cocktails and enjoy dishes such as garlic-rich prawns and clams.

4 Quinta do Serrado, Porto Santo
MAP L1 ▪ Hotel Quinta do Serrado, Sítio do Pedregal ▪ 291 980 270 ▪ €€€

This hotel-restaurant serves hearty fare, such as pork loin with bacon and coriander sauce. The passion fruit pudding is a delight. There is an excellent wine list.

5 Baiana, Vila Baleira
MAP L2 ▪ Rua Dr Nuno S Teixeira 9 ▪ 291 984 649 ▪ €€€

Join the locals at this popular seafood restaurant. Of the many types of fish caught and cooked each day, there's bound to be one you haven't tried.

6 Salinas, Vila Baleira
MAP L2 ▪ Rua Goulart Medeiros (part of the Torre Praia Hotel) ▪ 291 980 450 ▪ €€€

The signature dishes at this stylish oceanfront eatery include mixed grill kebab with banana and octopus stew.

7 Adega das Levadas, Miradouro das Flores
MAP K2 ▪ Sítio da Ponta-Morenos ▪ 291 982 721 ▪ €

This delightful, family-run place is known for its traditional food, much of it prepared using home-grown ingredients.

8 Panorama Restaurant & Lounge Bar, Casinhas
MAP L2 ▪ Estrada Carlos Pestana Vasconcelos ▪ 291 983 122 ▪ €€ ▪ Closed Mon

Seriously romantic views make dining here a special occasion.

Panorama Restaurant and its views

9 Casa d'Avó, Campo de Baixo
MAP L2 ▪ Estrada da Calheta ▪ 291 982 037 ▪ €

The homely ambience and the sense of humour displayed by staff ensure a relaxed and fun night out. The local wines are especially recommended.

10 Bar João do Cabeço
MAP L2 ▪ Sitio do Cabeço da Ponta ▪ 291 982 137 ▪ €

On the main ER111 road, this friendly, low-key café-restaurant is a popular local haunt, especially for lunch.

See map on p100

Streetsmart

An iconic blue-and-white ceramic tile
in Monte, Madeira

Getting To and Around Madeira

Arriving by Air

Madeira's main airport is **Cristiano Ronaldo International Airport**, 20 km (12 miles) from central Funchal, served by taxi and national and international car rental companies. **Tap Air Portugal** flies direct from Lisbon and Porto daily, and connects the island to major European hubs. **Azores Airlines** (SATA) operates scheduled flights between Funchal and Lisbon and Porto. **British Airways** has direct flights from selected UK airports, as do low-cost carriers **Jet2**, **EasyJet**, **Thomson Airways**, and **Thomas Cook Airlines**.

There are no direct connections from the US or Canada; instead, flights are routed through Lisbon or the Azores. Online travel agents, such as **Expedia**, are the fastest way to check flights and prices, as well as hotel and car-hire options.

Porto Santo Airport, in the centre of the island, is not served by public transport: the only way to get there from your hotel is by taxi. Taxis wait at the terminal when flights are due. There's also a shuttle bus service. Alternatively, reach your onward destination by arranging a pick-up in advance with a specialist airport transfer company such as **Madeira Airport Transfers**. This will save time and money.

Arriving by Sea

There are currently no ferries operating between the Portuguese mainland and Madeira. The island features on a number of cruise itineraries, but passengers usually spend only a few hours in port.

Getting Around by Bus

Buses are an economical and easy way of getting around the island, though services are geared to the peak commuter hours of 8–10am and 4–7pm. **Horários do Funchal** operates all urban services in the city, including wheelchair-friendly Linha Eco minibuses. It also serves selected (interurban) destinations in central Madeira including Santana (via Ribeiro Frio), Curral das Freiras and Camacha. For destinations further to the east, including Caniço, Santa Cruz and Machico, look for buses run by **SAM**, which also operates the Aerobus concession, or **EACL**, which additionally serves places such as Garajau. **Rodoeste** runs services to places west of Funchal, and to Porto Moniz and São Vicente on the north coast.

There is no central bus station in Funchal. Instead, buses depart from various points on the seafront (Avenida do Mar). Departure points for interurban routes can be found in the Zona Velha and many Rodoeste buses stop in the Hotel Zone (Lido).

Bus tickets can be bought from the driver. However, Horários do Funchal city buses need a Giro card, purchased from the driver or from machines set along the seafront. It costs 50c and should then be charged with cash for discounted travel. One- and three-day tickets are available.

Getting Around by Taxi

Madeira's yellow taxis are ubiquitous and convenient. In Funchal fares are metered. Journeys are unmetered outside the city. Determine the price beforehand, and don't be afraid to haggle. There are set prices for some pre-defined routes and these are displayed on the back of the driver's or front passenger's seat. The pick-up charge is €2.50 (€3 at night and weekends). You may also have to pay for excess baggage (wheelchairs are free of charge). You can also use companies such as **TaxiMadeira** to book private or personalised half- and whole-day tours of the island.

Getting Around by Car and Scooter

Hiring a car gives greater flexibility. However, be aware that parking in Funchal is difficult and metered. Underground car parks are the most convenient option. All international hire companies have airport and city-centre offices. Local car rental companies, such as **Rodavante** and **Auto Jardim**, often quote better deals. Hiring a scooter is a popular alternative for getting around but bear in mind Madeira's steep roads, hairpin bends and unpredictable weather.

Getting Around by Bicycle

Conventional bicycle hire options are limited, but visitors can opt for an electric bike for more relaxed touring and hill climbing. These bikes have an average range of about 25 km (16 miles). You can rent one at **E-Bike Madeira**. Mountain biking is also extremely popular: **Freeride Madeira** is a trusted local operator.

Porto Santo by Air

Aerovip operates daily flights at regular intervals to Porto Santo. The trip takes 25 minutes. Tickets can be purchased at any travel agent or booked online, and you can check in 48 hours before departure. Tickets cost around €150 return.

Porto Santo by Sea

Operated by **Porto Santo Line**, modern car ferries with cinema, restaurants and first- and second-class lounges run to Porto Santo. The journey takes two and a half hours.

Ships leave at 8am daily from Funchal. Return departure times depend on the day of the week and the season. Tickets for the ferry can be purchased online.

The Ilhas Desertas by Sea

Many non-scheduled tour services operate to the Ilhas Desertas ("Deserted Islands"). **Madeira Wind Birds** emphasise bird- and whale-watching. The guides on **Ventura** cruises are marine biologists and naturalists. Both tours depart from the marina at Funchal.

DIRECTORY

ARRIVING BY AIR

Azores Airlines
📞 707 227 282
🌐 sata.pt

British Airways
📞 217 616 144
🌐 britishairways.com

Cristiano Ronaldo International Airport
📞 291 520 700
🌐 ana.pt

EasyJet
📞 218 413 500
🌐 easyjet.com

Expedia
🌐 expedia.com

Jet2
📞 0333 300 0404
🌐 jet2.com

Madeira Airport Transfers
📞 913 756 539
🌐 madeira-airport-transfers.com

Porto Santo Airport
📞 291 520 700
🌐 ana.pt

Tap Air Portugal
📞 707 205 700
🌐 flytap.com

Thomas Cook Airlines
🌐 thomascookairlines.com

Thomson Airways
🌐 thomson.co.uk

GETTING AROUND BY BUS

EACL
📞 291 222 558
🌐 eacl.pt

Horários do Funchal
🌐 horariosdofunchal.pt

Rodoeste
🌐 rodoeste.com.pt

SAM
📞 291 201 151
🌐 sam.pt

GETTING AROUND BY TAXI

TaxiMadeira
📞 912 000 625
🌐 taximadeira.com

GETTING AROUND BY CAR AND SCOOTER

Auto Jardim
🌐 carhiremadeira.net

Rodavante
📞 291 742 448
🌐 rodavante.com

GETTING AROUND BY BICYCLE

E-Bike Madeira
📞 965 010 655
🌐 ebikemadeira.com

Freeride Madeira
📞 925 977 046
🌐 freeridemadeira.com

PORTO SANTO BY AIR

Aerovip
📞 291 106 976
🌐 aerovip.pt

PORTO SANTO BY SEA

Porto Santo Line
📞 291 210 300
🌐 portosantoline.pt

THE ILHAS DESERTAS BY SEA

Madeira Wind Birds
📞 917 777 441
🌐 madeirawindbirds.com

Ventura
📞 963 691 995
🌐 venturadomar.com

Practical Information

Passports and Visas

An autonomous region of Portugal, Madeira is a full member of the European Union (EU) and part of the Schengen Zone. Those not from the European Economic Area (EEA), EU and Switzerland will need a valid passport to enter. EEA, EU and Swiss citizens can use national identity cards instead. Visitors from Australia, New Zealand, the USA and Canada can stay for 90 days in any six months without a visa. Citizens of other countries should check with the nearest Portuguese embassy for entry and exit conditions. The website of the **Secretary of State for Portuguese Communities** states visa requirements. The **American** consulate in Funchal, and **British**, **Canadian** and **Australian** embassies in Lisbon provide consular services.

Customs and Immigration

There is virtually no limit on the amount of alcohol and tobacco you can bring in from EU countries for personal use. It is illegal to export scrimshaw and other items made from whale teeth and bone. The **Visa HQ** website outlines import/export limits for those travelling from outside the EU.

Travel Safety Advice

Visitors can get up-to-date travel safety information from the **UK Foreign and Commonwealth Office**, the **US Department of State** and the **Australian Department of Foreign Affairs and Trade**.

Travel Insurance

Take out travel insurance to cover private medical treatment, the loss or theft of belongings and cancelled or delayed flights. Adventure tourists should consider purchasing extra cover from companies such as **Essential Travel**.

All EU nations have reciprocal arrangements with Portugal for medical care and expenses, but dental care will probably have to be paid for. All EU and British citizens should ensure they carry their **EHIC** (European Health Insurance Card), for "necessary medical treatment". Apply for, or renew, the card online.

Health

Foreign visitors do not need any vaccinations, although arrivals from countries where yellow fever is prevalent will need proof of inoculation.

Healthcare facilities tend to be relatively basic outside the main towns. Walk-in health centres (centros de saúde) provide non-emergency treatment, but foreign visitors are most likely to be directed to an outpatient department at a hospital. Travel clinic websites such as **NaTHNac** are good sources of information. If extended medical treatment is required, confirm that the hospital or clinic accepts your insurance coverage.

Personal Security

Madeira is very safe for visitors, including solo women travellers. Never leave valuables unattended, however, and avoid leaving personal items in rental cars, even in the boot. The vehicles are easily recognized by would-be thieves.

To make an insurance claim, you will need to make an official police report; go to the **Funchal Police HQ**. Theft or loss of documents, such as a passport, should also be reported to your embassy.

Emergency Services

To contact the fire brigade (bombeiros), ambulance (ambulância) or police (polícia), dial the Europe-wide **emergency number**. Most operators should be able to speak English.

Travellers with Specific Needs

TAP Air Portugal, Azores Airlines (SATA) and other airlines offer in-flight and ground support with the MyWay service to those with mobility issues. Request this at the time of booking. **Accessible Portugal** specializes in tours for travellers with disabilities and can arrange hotel and airport transfers using vehicles adapted for wheelchairs. **Disabled Holidays** list hotel properties suitable for guests with limited mobility and also arrange travel insurance for those with disabilities and pre-existing medical conditions.

Most buses have disabled access, including Linha Eco minibuses. The cable car to Monte *(see pp34–5)* is also adapted.

Around 2 km (1 mile) of the Queimadas to Pico das Pedras trail is suitable for wheelchair use.

Currency and Banking

Portugal's currency is the euro. Euro banknotes come in denominations of €5, €10, €20, €50, €100, €200 and €500. Coins are 1c, 2c, 5c, 10c, 20c, 50c, €1 and €2. Banknotes of more than €50 are not widely circulated or easily accepted as payment for goods and services. The most convenient way to obtain funds is at an ATM, locally called Multibanco or MB. Check what charges are levied by your bank before you leave home. Most local banks and the airport **Unicâmbio** kiosk offer currency exchange. Travellers' cheques are no longer widely accepted.

Without a credit card, you cannot rent a car or check into a hotel. **Visa** and **MasterCard** are widely accepted, Diners Club and American Express less so. Note your card's global assistance numbers.

Telephone and Internet

Portugal's country code is 00351. Most public telephones only accept a prepaid phone card *(carta telefónico)*, available from post offices, newsagents and kiosks. Avoid using a hotel telephone as charges are high. Many hostels, guesthouses and hotels offer free Wi-Fi (guests are given a password). Free internet access is available at the airport and in bars, cafés and larger shopping malls.

To use your mobile phone here, it will need to be equipped for GSM frequencies 900 and 1800 MHz. EU tariffs apply. If staying two weeks or more, or to avoid high roaming fees, buy a Portuguese SIM card to use local rates. Check with your carrier whether you need to unlock your device to use a different SIM card/service.

DIRECTORY

PASSPORTS AND VISAS

American Consular Agency, Funchal
Rua da Alfândega 10, 2
☎ 291 235 636
ⓦ pt.usembassy.gov

Australian Embassy, Lisbon
Avenida da Liberdade 200
ⓦ portugal.embassy.gov.au

British Embassy, Lisbon
Rua de São Bernardo 33
☎ (021) 392 4000
ⓦ gov.uk

Canadian Embassy, Lisbon
Avenida da Liberdade 196
ⓦ portugal.gc.ca

Secretary of State for Portuguese Communities
ⓦ secomunidades.pt/vistos

CUSTOMS AND IMMIGRATION

Visa HQ
ⓦ portugal.visahq.com/customs

TRAVEL SAFETY ADVICE

Australian Department of Foreign Affairs and Trade
ⓦ dfat.gov.au
ⓦ smartraveller.go.au

UK Foreign and Commonwealth Office
ⓦ gov.uk/foreign-travel-advice

US Department of State
ⓦ travel.state.gov

TRAVEL INSURANCE

EHIC
ⓦ nhs.uk/ehic

Essential Travel
ⓦ essentialtravel.co.uk

HEALTH

NaTHNac
ⓦ nathnac.net

PERSONAL SECURITY

Funchal Police HQ
Rua da Infância 28
☎ 291 208 400

EMERGENCY SERVICES

Emergency Number
☎ 112

CURRENCY AND BANKING

MasterCard
☎ 080 096 4767 (UK)

Unicâmbio
Cristiano Ronaldo International Airport
☎ 966 982 184

Visa
☎ 800 811 824 (Portugal)

TRAVELLERS WITH SPECIFIC NEEDS

Accessible Portugal
ⓦ accessibleportugal.com

Disabled Holidays
ⓦ disabledholidays.com

Postal Services

The Portuguese postal service is called **CTT Correios de Portugal**. *Correios* (post offices) are usually open 8:30am–8pm on weekdays and 9am–1pm on Saturdays. First-class mail is *correio azul*; second-class is *normal*. *Correio azul* should be posted in blue postboxes, and everything else within red postboxes. Funchal's main post office is **Correios Avenida Gonçalves Zarco**.

Opening Hours

Shops are generally open 9am–1pm and 2–6pm Monday–Friday, and 9am–1:30pm Saturday. In the main towns, larger stores often stay open through lunch. Shopping centres and malls in Funchal, such as **Forum Madeira** *(see p77)*, usually open 10am–11pm Monday–Friday and till midnight at weekends and on holidays. In rural areas, expect shops to close at weekends.

Banking hours are 8:30am–3pm Monday–Friday. Museums generally open 10am–12:30pm and 2–6pm. Some close on Mondays.

Time Difference

Madeira keeps Greenwich Mean Time (GMT). Clocks move forward an hour during daylight saving time, from the last Sunday in March until the last Sunday in October, when they move back an hour.

Electrical Appliances

Portugal uses plugs with two round pins and an electrical mains voltage of 220V/50Hz. US visitors will need a plug adaptor and a converter, while those from other regions may require only a plug adaptor – check ahead. Most hotel bathrooms offer built-in adaptors for electric razors.

Weather

Christmas and New Year are peak periods, with room rates considerably higher. Easter, Carnaval (February or March), July and August are also busy. June can be surprisingly quiet, and enjoys near perfect weather. Madeira has a mild, subtropical climate, with average temperatures ranging from 17° C (62° F) in February to 23° C (75° F) in September. October to March has the highest rainfall, especially on the northern side of the island. Porto Santo tends to be fine all year round.

Visitor Information

Funchal's main **Tourist Information Office** is on Avenida Arriaga. The **Visit Madeira** website is a useful source of information, with lists of tourist offices, approved accommodation and suggestions on where to go and what to do. Other useful websites include **Madeira-Web**, the **Madeira Promotion Bureau**, **Madeira Island Direct** and the **Madeira Island News** blog. Online magazine **Madeira Live** includes a live webcam stream from Funchal. **The Best of Madeira** is a free guide to restaurants, bars and other attractions and includes discount vouchers. Readers can also download its free app.

Shopping

Traditional Madeiran souvenirs include lace and embroidery *(see pp64–5)*. Local pieces are checked for quality and marked with a hologram tag and, in some cases, by a lead seal. Shoes and leather goods are popular Portuguese specialities and Madeira is known for its hard-wearing ankle boots and stylish leather sandals. You can watch them being handcrafted at the **Mercado dos Lavradores** *(see pp24–5)*.

If you are taking home some of the island's beautiful flowers, ask the florist to deliver them to your hotel on the morning of your departure, packed in a robust cardboard container. Beware, however, that if these boxes exceed the dimensions for hand baggage, these boxes may be regarded as hold luggage and will attract an excess charge.

Good quality Madeira wine *(see pp62–3)* should have Sercial, Verdelho or Malvasia on the label to show that it is of high quality and made by traditional methods, using the classic grape varieties. Another souvenir with a long history is *aguardente* (a strong alcoholic spirit), often described as rum. White *aguardentes* are commonly served as *poncha*, mixed with honey and lemon. Aged, dark *aguardentes* are after-dinner drinks with real character and flavour.

Non-EU residents can

claim back VAT (IVA in Portuguese) on purchases over €61.35. **Global Blue** has more details.

Dining

Madeira is fast becoming one of Portugal's gourmet hotspots. Traditionally, Madeiran cuisine has focused on fish and seafood. Menu favourites are juicy *bifes de atum* (tuna steaks) and intensely flavoured *lapas* (limpets), served grilled on the half shells with garlic butter and a slice of lemon. Don't miss the mouthwatering local *peixe espada* (scabbard fish) with fried banana, or *espetada*, sizzling grilled skewers of quality poultry and meats *(see p61)*.

A lot of the island's best restaurants are housed in hotels, which can mean a smart casual dress code. Expect to pay a premium for the experience. Otherwise the majority of eateries across the island are wonderfully informal and reasonably priced, with many being family-run. For an inexpensive meal, order the *prato do dia* (dish of the day). Invariably wholesome and served quickly, this is the plate of choice for ordinary, working Portuguese. If you're not very hungry but still prefer a meal to a snack, ask for a *meia dose* or *mini-prato* (half portion).

There's nearly always a children's menu and some restaurants can provide high chairs, though check ahead. All restaurants are non-smoking, although tables on outside terraces are exempt from this rule.

Tipping is not customary, but if you feel the food and service are exceptional 10 per cent of the total is more than enough.

Accommodation

In Madeira, location has a big influence on price. City-centre hotels are far less expensive than the luxurious five-star hotels located on the Estrada Monumental in the west of Funchal. Prices fall the further you go from the city centre and the sea.

Rural properties and country hotels frequently boast converted agricultural buildings that have been turned into self-contained cottages or villas. **Madeira Rural** lists around 20 such options. *Estalagens* and *pousadas* (inns) or *quintas* (manor houses) are hotels with great historic character, often set on an estate with gardens. **Charming Hotels Madeira** offers various options. **Madeira Apartments** lists hotel and private apartments in a variety of locations.

Bed and breakfast options come in the form of *pensões* or *residencias*, which are clean, basic guesthouses. Private home rentals are available on **Airbnb**. Budget travellers can find hostels in and around Funchal. **Hostel World** lists the most popular options.

The only campsite, Parque de Campismo do Porto Moniz, is located in Ribeira da Janela. There is additional camping on Porto Santo in Fontinha, right by the beach. The Visit Madeira website has more details.

DIRECTORY

POSTAL SERVICES

Correios Avenida Gonçalves Zarco
Avenida G Zarco 9, Funchal
☎ 291 202 830

CTT Correios de Portugal
🌐 ctt.pt

VISITOR INFORMATION

Madeira Island Direct
🌐 madeiraislanddirect.com

Madeira Island News
🌐 madeiraislandnews.com

Madeira Live
🌐 madeira-live.com

Madeira Promotion Bureau
🌐 apmadeira.pt

Madeira-Web
🌐 madeira-web.com

The Best of Madeira
🌐 bestguide.pt

Tourist Information Office
Avenida Arriaga 16 ■ Open 9am–8pm Mon–Sat, 9am–3:30pm weekends and public holidays
☎ 291 211 902
🌐 visitmadeira.pt

Visit Madeira
🌐 visitmadeira.pt

SHOPPING

Global Blue
🌐 globalblue.com

ACCOMMODATION

Airbnb
🌐 airbnb.com

Charming Hotels Madeira
🌐 charming-hotels-madeira.com

Hostel World
🌐 hostelworld.com

Madeira Apartments
🌐 madeiraapartments.com

Madeira Rural
🌐 madeirarural.com

Places to Stay

PRICE CATEGORIES
For a standard double room per night (with breakfast if included), taxes and extra charges.

€ under €100   €€ €100-€200   €€€ over €200

Resort Hotels

Meliá Madeira Mare
MAP G6 ▪ Rua de Leichlingen, Funchal 9000-003 ▪ 291 724 140 ▪ www.melia.com ▪ €€
A spectacular lagoon-pool and state-of-the-art spa are at this upscale resort hotel. A unique experience is the Chef In Your Kitchen service – a private dinner prepared in your room.

Pestana Grand
MAP G6 ▪ Rua da Ponte da Cruz 23, Funchal 9000-103 ▪ 291 707 400 ▪ www.pestana.com ▪ €€
On Ponta da Cruz headland west of Funchal, the Grand boasts an outdoor pool complex, with seawater meandering through beautiful tropical gardens and swaying palms.

Savoy Saccharum
MAP B4 ▪ Rua Serra de Água 1, Arco da Calheta 9370-083 ▪ 291 820 800 ▪ www. savoyresortscom ▪ €€
Overlooking Calheta's marina is a trendy retreat designed by Nini Andrade Silva. The island's sugar cane industry is a theme in the Engenho restaurant.

Pestana Porto Santo
MAP L2 ▪ Estrada Regional 120, Sitio do Campo de Baixo, Porto Santo 9400-242 ▪ 291 144 000 ▪ www.pestana.com ▪ €€€
This all-inclusive beach resort features one- and two-bedroom suites and poolside villas. Breakfast, lunch, dinner, snacks and national drinks are all included in room rates. There are comprehensive on-site leisure facilities.

Reid's Palace
MAP G6 ▪ Estrada Monumental 139, Funchal 9000-098 ▪ 291 717 171 ▪ www.belmond.com ▪ €€€
World-renowned Reid's has the feel of a country manor house – antiques and works of art at every turn, gardens with pools, and terrific views. A spa and the Michelin-starred William restaurant (see p79) add to the allure.

Royal Savoy
MAP H6 ▪ Rua Carvalho Araújo, Funchal 9000-022 ▪ 291 213 500 ▪ www. hotelroyalsavoymadeira. com ▪ €€€
Elegantly furnished and themed around Portugal's Age of Discovery, the Royal Savoy makes use of its Atlantic Ocean overlook, with grounds and pools filled by lush, subtropical flora.

The Cliff Bay
MAP G6 ▪ Estrada Monumental 147, Funchal 9004-532 ▪ 291 707 700 ▪ www.portobay.com ▪ €€€
Surrounded by beautiful terraced gardens leading to palm-shaded pools, this fabulous oceanfront property houses the two-Michelin-starred Il Gallo d'Oro restaurant (see p79). Guest wellbeing extends to a luxury spa.

Character Hotels

Funchal Design Hotel
MAP P1 ▪ Rua da Alegria 2, 9000-040 Funchal ▪ 291 780 210 ▪ www.funchal designhotel.pt ▪ €
Sleek, quirky interior with printed fabrics and black-and-white photographs. A short distance to the town centre. Some rooms have kitchenettes.

Casa Velha do Palheiro
MAP H5 ▪ Rua da Estalagem 28, São Gonçalo, Funchal 9060-415 ▪ 291 790 350 ▪ www.casa-velha.com ▪ €€
Celebrated for its gardens (see pp22–3) and excellent golf course (see p57), the 200-year-old Casa Velha also has a noted restaurant and boutique spa.

Casino Park Hotel
MAP Q1 ▪ Rua Imperatriz Dona Amélia, Funchal 9004-513 ▪ 291 209 100 ▪ www.pestana.com ▪ €€
Designed by renowned Brazilian architect Oscar Niemeyer, the hotel has nightlife including dinner dances and professional cabaret. Guests can access glitzy Casino da Madeira.

Castanheiro Boutique Hotel
MAP P3 ▪ Rua do Castanheiro 31, Funchal 9000-081 ▪ 291 200 100 ▪ www.castanheiroboutique hotel.com ▪ €€
In the heart of Funchal's old quarter, this 81-room bolthole comprises five

historic buildings spanning 300 years. Antiques and period furniture decorate the hotel's interior, but the rooftop infinity pool is a thoroughly modern perk.

Porto Santa Maria

MAP Q5 ▪ Avenida do Mar e das Comunidades Madeirenses 50, Funchal 9060-190 ▪ 291 206 700 ▪ www.portobay.com ▪ €€
An adult-only hotel sited on the water's edge just a few minutes' walk from the old town. Guests enjoy exclusive harbour views, and leisure amenities of indoor and outdoor pools, plus a lovely spa.

Quinta da Bela Vista

MAP G6 ▪ Caminho do Avista Navios 4, São Martinho, Funchal 9000-129 ▪ 291 706 400 ▪ www.belavistamadeira.com ▪ €€
The "Beautiful View" is of the wild cliffs to the east, but it could describe the lovely gardens of this traditional manor house.

Quinta da Casa Branca

MAP G6 ▪ Rua da Casa Branca 7, Funchal 9000-088 ▪ 291 700 770 ▪ www.quintacasabranca.com ▪ €€
While the manor house retains its 19th-century ambience, rooms in the modern wing are cleverly integrated into the gardens, filled with exotic trees.

Quinta das Vistas

MAP H5 ▪ Caminho de Santo António 52, Funchal 9000-187 ▪ 291 750 007 ▪ www.quintadasvistasmadeira.com ▪ €€
As its name suggests, this carefully renovated

1930s-style manor house affords fabulous views over Funchal. The palm-fringed public areas and spruce gardens lend it a pleasant colonial air.

Quinta do Monte

MAP H5 ▪ Caminho do Monte 192-194, Monte, Funchal 9050-288 ▪ 291 780 100 ▪ www.quintadomontemadeira.com ▪ €€
A calm oasis, high above Funchal in a lush, walled garden. The manor at the heart of the estate is set with antique furniture and oriental rugs.

Quinta Mirabela

MAP H5 ▪ Caminho do Monte 105-107, Funchal 9050-288 ▪ 291 780 210 ▪ www.quinta-mirabela.com ▪ €€
The original building from 1888 has been sensitively refurbished with a contemporary design that melds old with new. The panoramic terrace is the place to enjoy tasty local and international cuisine.

Quinta Perestrello

MAP G6 ▪ Rua Dr Pita 3, Funchal 9000-089 ▪ 291 706 700 ▪ www.quintaperestrellomadeira .com ▪ €€
Set in mature gardens, this charming heritage hotel is a fine example of the elegant homes of Madeira's prominent merchants. The traditional restaurant includes regional gastronomy.

The Vine

MAP P2 ▪ Rua das Aranhas 27, Funchal 9000-044 ▪ 291 009 000 ▪ www.hotelthevine.com ▪ €€
With its stylish and daringly inventive

interiors, this modern city-centre property oozes sophistication. The spa menu lists Madeira wine massage among other options. A plunge pool and the UVA restaurant (see p79) crown the roof.

Pestana CR7

MAP Q2 ▪ Avenida Sá Carneiro-Praça do Mar, Funchal 9000-017 ▪ 291 140 480 ▪ www.pestanacr7.com ▪ €€€
Named for Portuguese footballer Cristiano Ronaldo and his number 7 shirt, an overnight here is an experience where all areas offer total digital convenience. There is a rooftop infinity pool and fine restaurant.

Hotels in Central Madeira

Estalagem Eira do Serrado

MAP G4 ▪ Curral das Freiras 9000-421 ▪ 291 710 060 ▪ www.eiradoserrado.com ▪ €
This mountain retreat is a great base from which to hike around the surrounding area. Guests are afforded spectacular views of the Curral das Freiras (see pp36-7) and its encircling cliffs.

Monte Mar Palace

MAP F2 ▪ Sítio do Montado, nr Ponta Delgada 9240-104 ▪ 291 860 030 ▪ www.montemarpalace.com ▪ €
At this hotel, which stands on a secluded bluff on the island's central northern coast, guests can enjoy fine Atlantic Ocean and mountain views. Leisure facilities include a pool, a pitch and putt course and a gravel court for pétanque.

Quinta da Serra

MAP F5 ▪ Estrada do Chote 4, Jardim da Serra 9325-140 ▪ 291 640 120 ▪ www.hotelquintadaserra.com ▪ €

Set amid leafy grounds, among organically grown crops, this beautifully renovated farmhouse offers modern and well-maintained rooms with views of the garden or of the distant sea.

Solar de Boaventura

MAP G2 ▪ Sítio do Serrão, Boaventura 9240-046 ▪ 291 860 888 ▪ www.solar-boaventura.com ▪ €

Tastefully converted from a classic Madeira house dating from 1776. Large rooms and a restaurant serving local specialities. Near the UNESCO-listed *laurissilva* forest (see p29).

Quinta do Estreito

MAP F5 ▪ Rua José Joaquim da Costa, Estreito de Câmara de Lobos 9325-034 ▪ 291 910 530 ▪ www.quinta doestreitomadeira.com ▪ €€

Once the area's main wine estate, the old house now holds the Adega da Quinta (see p85) and Bacchus restaurants. Modern guest quarters are set in landscaped gardens.

Quinta do Furão

MAP H2 ▪ Estrada Quinta do Furão 6, Santana 9230-082 ▪ 291 570 100 ▪ www.quintadofurao.com ▪ €€

Rooms at this traditionally styled but luxuriously modern hotel enjoy views along the rugged north coast. Set on a headland near Santana, the hotel is noted for its excellent restaurant (see p85).

Hotels in Eastern Madeira

Cais da Oliveira

MAP J6 ▪ Caminho Cais da Oliveira, Caniço de Baixo 9125-028 ▪ 291 934 991 ▪ www.rocamarlido resorts.com ▪ €

Seemingly sculpted from the clifftop, the hotel's rooms and suites are arranged around indoor and outdoor pools, a restaurant and terraces facing a crystal blue ocean.

Four Views Oasis

MAP J5 ▪ Praia dos Reis Magos, Caniço 9125-024 ▪ 291 930 100 ▪ www.fourviewshotels.com ▪ €

Hugely popular and good value, this waterfront option can arrange all sorts of leisure activity packages. The popular Praia dos Reis Magos (see p53) is on the doorstep.

Porto Bay Serra Golf

MAP J4 ▪ Sítio dos Casais Próximos, Santa Cruz 9100-255 ▪ 291 550 500 ▪ www.portobay.com ▪ €

A short stroll from Santo da Serra Golf Course (see p56), this charming place offers a covered pool, spa, gym and library. The Avó Micas restaurant (see p99) is definitely worth trying.

White Waters

MAP K4 ▪ Praceta 25 de Abril 34, Machico 9200-084 ▪ 291 969 380 ▪ www.whitewaters-madeira.com ▪ €

Located near the airport, this family-run boutique option with modern architecture has ocean-view rooms. Guests can dine at the restaurant or unwind on the terrace. Machico's sandy beach (see p52) is nearby.

Galosol

MAP J5 ▪ Ponta da Oliveira, Caniço 9125-031 ▪ 291 930 930 ▪ www.galoresort.com ▪ €€

The emphasis here is on active tourism, with outdoor yoga, jogging and kayaking among other pastimes. But there are also two pools, a spa and plenty of opportunities to do nothing at all.

Quinta Splendida

MAP J5 ▪ Estrada Ponta da Oliveira 11, Caniço 9125-001 ▪ 291 930 400 ▪ www.quintasplendida.com ▪ €€

Tucked away in beautiful botanical gardens, this 19th-century restored manor has 141 traditional rooms, 25 spa suites and three restaurants. The hotel spa is one of the largest in Madeira.

Albatroz Beach & Yacht Club

MAP K5 ▪ Quinta Dr Américo Durao, Sítio da Terça, Santa Cruz 9100-187 ▪ 291 520 290 ▪ www.albatrozhotel.com ▪ €€€

This 15-room boutique hotel mixes a preppy maritime look with trad-itional island motifs, and a sense of exclusivity. The fresh- and seawater pools are enticing, the exotic gardens delightful and the restaurant tempting.

Hotels in Western Madeira

Estalagem do Vale

MAP E2 ▪ Sítio das Feiteiras de Baixo, São Vicente 9240-206 ▪ 291 840 160 ▪ www.estalagemdovale.com ▪ €

A historical country-style inn in UNESCO-protected

laurissilva forest *(see p29)* this gem has its own pool and spa. The restaurant is noted for its haute cuisine.

Hotel Encumeada

MAP E4 ▪ Feiteiras-Serra de Água 9350-000 ▪ 291 951 282 ▪ www.hotel encumeada.com ▪ €
With fine mountain views and amid laurel forest, this large chalet-style hotel is close to some of the best *levada* and mountain paths on the island.

Pousada dos Vinháticos

MAP E4 ▪ Serra de Água, Ribeira Brava 9350-306 ▪ 291 952 344 ▪ www. dorisol.com ▪ €
This small country inn sits between two of the island's majestic groups of mountains. End the day with drinks on the terrace admiring the peaks.

Aqua Natura

MAP C1 ▪ Rotunda da Piscina 3, Porto Moniz 9270-156 ▪ 291 640 100 ▪ www.aquanatura madeira. com ▪ €€
Bright blues and lime greens lend the interior of this spruce, family-friendly hotel a refreshingly light and easy character. Sited very near to the natural rock pools *(see p53)*.

Estalagem Ponta do Sol

MAP D5 ▪ Quinta da Rochina, Ponta do Sol 9360-529 ▪ 291 970 200 ▪ www.pontadosol.com ▪ €€
Enjoy views of the setting sun from this stylish clifftop hotel. Distinctive bridges and towers link modern guest quarters with the more traditional public areas, including a glass-walled restaurant.

Jardim Atlântico

MAP B3 ▪ Lombo da Rocha, Prazeres 9370-605 ▪ 291 820 220 ▪ www. jardimatlantico.com ▪ €€
The remoteness of this hotel is part of its charm. Guests can explore the surrounding coast and countryside. Apartments, studios, and bungalows are huge, and there is a mini-market on site.

Savoy Calheta Beach

MAP B4 ▪ Vila da Calheta, Calheta 9370-133 ▪ 291 820 300 ▪ www.savoy calhetabeach.com ▪ €€
Set overlooking Calheta's sandy beach *(see p52)* this stylish hotel has the feel of a Mediterranean resort. The rooms, suites and apartments are located around an inviting outdoor pool, and there are a couple of good eateries on the premises.

Guesthouses and B&Bs

Albergaria Catedral

MAP P3 ▪ Rua do Aljube 13, Funchal 9000-067 ▪ 291 230 091 ▪ €
Original furnishings from the early 20th century define the interior of this no-frills budget option. Its location is spot on, right in front of the cathedral. Enjoy breakfast on the top-floor panoramic terrace.

Casa do Velho Dragoeiro

MAP L2 ▪ Rua Gregorio Pestana 16a, Vila Baleira, Porto Santo 9400-172 ▪ 291 634 413 ▪ www. casadovelhodragoeiro. com ▪ €
This hotel is simply but attractively furnished. Guests can retreat behind stone walls and soak in

the pool. One of the best budget options on Porto Santo. Be sure to book ahead for August.

Hotel Salgueira

MAP B1 ▪ Lugar do Tenente 34, Porto Moniz 9270-095 ▪ 291 850 080 ▪ www.hotelsalgueiro. com ▪ €
Upgraded from *pensão* to hotel, Salgueira remains charming and hospitable. Rooms and suites have been renovated, and the restaurant still appeals.

Residencial Amparo

MAP K4 ▪ Rua da Amargura, Machico 9200-085 ▪ 291 968 120 ▪ www.amparohotel.com ▪ €
Acclaimed interior designer Nini Andrade Silva decorated this light and airy guesthouse and its 12 rooms. The restaurant serves hearty Madeiran fare.

Residencial da Mariazinha

MAP P5 ▪ Rua de Santa Maria 155, Funchal 9000-040 ▪ 291 220 239 ▪ www.residencial mariazinha.com ▪ €
Located in Funchal's oldest street, which is attractively cobbled and buzzing with life at night, this lovely inn has five rooms plus one suite with its own Jacuzzi.

Vila Teresinha

MAP N1 ▪ Rua das Cruzes 21, Funchal 9000-025 ▪ 291 741 723 ▪ www. vilateresinha.com ▪ €
Friendly, family-run guesthouse, where some of the rooms have private balconies with views of Funchal. Near the Museu da Quinta das Cruzes.

Index

Acknowledgments

Author

Christopher Catling has written more than 50 travel guides, including best-selling DK *Eyewitness* guides to Florence and Venice. When not writing books, he works as an archaeologist and heritage consultant. He is a Fellow of the Society of Antiquaries and the Royal Society of Arts, and a member of the British Guild of Travel Writers. He loves Madeira, and never tires of visiting it to walk and to enjoy the food and warm hospitality of the islanders.

Special thanks for the invaluable assistance of the Madeira Tourist Board in Funchal, the Madeira Promotion Bureau and the Portuguese National Tourist Office in London.

Additional contributor
Paul Bernhardt

Publishing Director Georgina Dee

Publisher Vivien Antwi

Design Director Phil Ormerod

Editorial Ankita Awasthi Tröger, Rachel Fox, Maresa Manera, Scarlett O'Hara, Sands Publishing Solutions, Sally Schafer, Hollie Teague, Rachel Thompson

Cover Design Richard Czapnik

Design Tessa Bindloss, Hansa Babra

Picture Research Taiyaba Khatoon, Ellen Root, Rituraj Singh

Cartography Zafar-ul-Islam Khan, James Macdonald, Casper Morris, John Plumer

Madeira base map derived from Madeira Tourist Board, www.visitmadeira.pt

DTP Jason Little

Production Igrain Roberts

Factchecker Marc di Duca

Proofreader Leena Lane

Indexer Hilary Bird

First edition produced by DP Services, a division of DUNCAN PETERSEN PUBLISHING LTD, 31 Ceylon Road, London W14 0PY

Commissioned Photography Kellie Walsh

Picture Credits

The publisher would like to thank the following for their kind permission to reproduce their photographs:
Key: a-above; b-below/bottom; c-centre; f-far; l-left; r-right; t-top

123RF.com: catafratto 4cla; Wiesław Jarek 97cla; Erich Teister 68cla.

Alamy Stock Photo: age fotostock 64br; Arco Images GmbH 89bl; Art Collection 2 19br; K J Bennett 37tr; Paul Bernhardt 23tl, 101b; Bildagentur-online / Sunny Celeste 24t; Philip Bird 56bl; Richard Bond 32–3, 38cla; Nigel Cattlin 2tl, 8–9; Clearview 45br; clive thompson travel 37crb; Maurice Crooks 11tl; Park Dale 34br; Martin A. Doe 44ccl; Roger Eritja 25tr; Doug Houghton Eur 27tl; eye35.pix 1; Stephen Frost 78tl; Hackenberg-Photo-Cologne 18bc; Hemis 39tl, 51cl, 55cl; George Hopkins 30–31; Ian Dagnall Commercial Collection 16br; Iconotec 6cla, 12bl; imageBROKER 10bl, 26bc, 46t; islandspics 44b; Karol Kozlowski Premium RM Collection 62b, 101tr; David Kilpatrick 91br; kpzfoto 104tc; Ian Littlewood 11clb; LOOK Die Bildagentur der Fotografen GmbH 33br; Vaclav Mach 73tr; Cro Magnon 63tr; mauritius images GmbH 55br; McCanner 45tl; Graham Mulrooney 35cl; Nature Picture Library 98tl; North Wind Picture Archives 42cl; Pictures Colour Library 74b; Pixel Prints 104br; Prisma by Dukas Presseagentur GmbH 4cl; Purple Marbles Madeira 48tl; Radius Images 23cr; Paul Shawcross 39crb, 64cla; Ian Smith 32clb; P Tomlins 3tr, 106–7; Tromp Willem van Urk 24bl; Sebastian Wasek 33tl; David Wingate 67tr; Jan Wlodarczyk 92–3; Zoonar GmbH 16cla.

AWL Images: Mauricio Abreu 87tr; Peter Adams 96b; ImageBROKER 20t.

Beef and Wines: 79br.

Casa Museu Frederico de Freitas, Funchal: 48b.

Dreamstime.com: 3quarks 4crb; Albertoloyo 4t; Aldorado10 11b, 49cl, 54b, 82–3, 84tr, 84clb, 87b; Steve Allen 35tl; Andersastphoto 28tl; Anitasstudio 2tr, 4clb, 34c, 40–41, 59br, 68b; Anphotos 29tc; Arbaes 4cr; Kushnirov Avraham 80tl; Marilyn Barbone 57tr; Marcel Van Den Bos 12–13, 22bl; Alena Brozova 29bl; Jiri Castka 7tr; Clickos 10crb, 18cla, 19cl, 72tl, 75cla, 76b; Coplandj 102bl; Henner Damke 3tl, 70–71; Dobs65 95b; Aleksandra Durdyn 53tr; Dziewul 54tl, 94cla; Morten Ekstroem 102t; Finaldream 77tr, 86ca; Armando Frazão 66–7, 100ca; Elena Frolova 25bl; Darren Howe 83cl; Nigel Hoy 90cl; Ihb 17tl; Wieslaw Jarek 13tl; Bernd Kelichhaus 51tr, 96ca; Anna Lurye 38–9, 52bl, 82cl; Alexander Mychko 61tr; Photonics 43tr; Saiko3p 10cla, 11tr, 13br, 36cl, 50b; Sandra 4b; Denis Shikov 27bl; John Silva 47cr; Merten Snijders 53clb; Rechitan Sorin 26–7; Nikolai Sorokin 58cla; T.w. Van Urk 58br; Zhykharievavlada 65br.

Getty Images: AFP / Gregorio Cunha 59tl; Henri Bureau 43cla; Luis Davilla 63clb; DEA /

G. Dagli Orti 42br; Simeone Huber 7br, 52t; Holger Leue 46bc, 65tl, 69cl, 85br; Frank Lukasseck 28b.

Il Gallo d'Oro: 60t, 79ca.

iStockphoto.com: aqualuso 11crb; Juergen Sack 88–9; saiko3p 81b.

Museu de Arte Sacra do Funchal: 10clb, 14c, 14bc, 15tl, 15c, 15crb, 15bl.

Panorama Restaurant: 105crb.

Quinta do Fura ão: 61bl.

Quinta Splendida Wellness & Botanical Garden: 99br.

Robert Harding Picture Library: Factoria Singular 16–17; Christian Handl 21cr, 21bl; Michael Jenner 50tc; Michael Nolan 81cr; Ellen Rooney 11cra.

SuperStock: age fotostock 49tr, 69tr; age fotostock / Karol Kozlowski 95tr, 103bl, / Mauro Tandoi 17crb, / Sebastian Wasek 22–3, 36–7, 66tl; Hemis.fr / Franck Guiziou 36br; imageBROKER 78c, / imageb / Norbert Probst 57clb, /Stefan Kiefer 88clb; Westend61 56tr.

Cover

Front and spine: Alamy Stock Photo: Jan Wlodarczyk

Back: **Dreamstime.com:** Ekaterina Pokrovsky

Pull Out Map Cover
Alamy Stock Photo: Jan Wlodarczyk

All other images © Dorling Kindersley
For further information see:
www.dkimages.com

Penguin
Random
House

Printed and bound in China

First American Edition, 2005
Published in the United States by
DK Publishing, 345 Hudson Street,
New York, New York 10014

Copyright 2005, 2018 ©
Dorling Kindersley Limited

A Penguin Random House Company

18 19 20 21 10 9 8 7 6 5 4 3 2 1

**Reprinted with revisions
2007, 2009, 2011, 2013, 2015, 2018**

Published in Great Britain
by Dorling Kindersley Limited.

A catalog record for this book is available
from the Library of Congress.

ISSN 1479-344X
ISBN 978 1 4654 6880 2

MIX
Paper from
responsible sources
FSC™ C018179

As a guide to abbreviations in visitor information blocks: **Adm** = admission charge.

Phrase Book

In an Emergency

Help!	Socorro!	soo-koh-roo
Stop!	Páre!	pahr'
Call a doctor!	Chame um médico!	shahm' ooñ meh-dee-koo
Call an ambulance!	Chame uma ambulância!	shahm' oo-muh añ-boo-lañ-see-uh
Call the police!	Chame a polícia!	shahm' uh poo-lee-see-uh
Call the fire brigade!	Chame os bombeiros!	shahm' oosh bom-bay-roosh

Communication Essentials

Yes	Sim	seeñ
No	Não	nowñ
Please	Por favor/ Faz favor	poor fuh-vor fash fuh-vor
Thank you	Obrigado/da	o-bree-gah-doo/duh
Excuse me	Desculpe	dish-koolp'
Hello	Olá	oh-lah
Goodbye	Adeus	a-deh-oosh
Yesterday	Ontem	oñ-tayñ
Today	Hoje	ohj'
Tomorrow	Amanhã	ah-man yañ
Here	Aqui	uh-kee
There	Ali	uh-lee
What?	O quê?	oo keh
Which?	Qual?	kwahl'
When?	Quando?	kwañ-doo
Why?	Porquê?	poor-keh
Where?	Onde?	oñd'

Useful Phrases

How are you?	Como está?	koh-moo shtah
Very well, thank you.	Bem, obrigado/da.	bayñ o-bree-gah-doo/duh
Where is/are…?	Onde está/ estão?	ond' shtah/ shtowñ
How far is it to…?	A que distância fica…?	uh kee dish-tañ-see-uh fee-kuh
Which way to…?	Como se vai para…?	koh-moo seh vy puh-ruh
Do you speak English?	Fala Inglês?	fah-luh eeñ-glehsh
I'm sorry.	Desculpe.	dish-koolp'
Could you speak more slowly please?	Pode falar mais devagar por favor?	pohd' fuh-lar mysh d'-va-gar poor fah-vor

Useful Words

big	grande	grand'
small	pequeno	pe-keh-noo
hot	quente	kent'
cold	frio	free-oo
good	bom	boñ
bad	mau	mah-oo
open	aberto	a-behr-too
closed	fechado	fe-shah-doo
left	esquerda	shkehr-duh
right	direita	dee-ray-tuh
straight on	em frente	ayñ frent'
near	perto	pehr-too
far	longe	loñj'
up	suba	soo-bah
down	desça	deh-shuh
early	cedo	seh-doo
late	tarde	tard'

entrance	entrada	en-trah-duh
exit	saída	sa-ee-duh
toilets	casa de banho	kah-zuh d' ban-yoo
more	mais	mysh
less	menos	meh-noosh

Shopping

How much does this cost?	Quanto custa isto?	kwan-too koosh-tuh eesh-too
I would like …	Queria …	kree-uh
I'm just looking.	Estou só a ver obrigado/a.	shtoh soh uh vehr o-bree-gah-doo/uh
Do you take credit cards?	Aceita cartões de crédito?	uh-say-tuh kar-toinsh de kreh-dee-too
What time do you open?	A que horas abre?	uh kee oh-rash ah-bre?
What time do you close?	A que horas fecha?	uh kee oh-rash fay-shuh?
this/that one	este/esse	ehst'/ehss'
expensive	caro	kah-roo
cheap	barato	buh-rah-too
size	número	noom'-roo
white	branco	brañ-koo
black	preto	preh-too
red	roxo	roh-shoo
yellow	amarelo	uh-muh-reh-loo
green	verde	vehrd'
blue	azul	uh-zool'
bakery	padaria	pah-duh-ree-uh
bank	banco	bañ-koo
bookshop	livraria	lee-vruh-ree-uh
cake shop	pastelaria	pash-te-luh-ree-uh
chemist	farmácia	far-mah-see-uh
market	mercado	mehr-kah-doo
newsagent	kiosque	kee-yohsk'
post office	correios	koo-ray-oosh

Sightseeing

cathedral	sé	seh
church	igreja	ee-gray-juh
garden	jardim	jar-deeñ
library	biblioteca	bee-blee-oo-teh-kuh
museum	museu	moo-zeh-oo
tourist information	posto de turismo	posh-too d' too-reesh-moo
bus station	estação de autocarros	shta-sowñ d' oh-too-kah-roosh
railway station	estação de comboios	shta-sowñ d' koñ-boy-oosh

Staying in a Hotel

Do you have a vacant room?	Tem um quarto livre?	tayñ ooñ kwar-too leevr'
room with a bath	um quarto com casa de banho	ooñ kwar-too koñ kah-zuh d' ban-yoo
shower	duche	doosh
single room	quarto individual	kwar-too een-dee-vee-doo-ahl'
double room	quarto de casal	kwar-too d' kuh-zhal'
twin room	quarto com duas camas	kwar-too koñ doo-ash kah-mash
I have a reservation.	Tenho um quarto reservado.	tayn-yoo ooñ kwar-too re-ser-vah-doo

Eating Out

Have you got a table for …?	Tem uma mesa para … ?	tayñ oo-muh meh-zuh puh-ruh
I'd like to reserve a table.	Quero reservar una mesa.	keh-roo re-zehr-var oo-muh meh-zuh
The bill, please.	A conta por favor/faz favor.	uh kohn-tuh poor fuh-vor/ fash fuh-vor
I am a vegetarian.	Sou vegetariano/a.	Soh ve-je-tuh-ree-ah-noo/uh
the menu	a lista	uh leesh-tuh
wine list	a lista de vinhos	uh leesh-tuh de veen-yoosh
glass	um copo	ooñ koh-poo
bottle	uma garrafa	oo-muh gar-rah-fuh
knife	uma faca	oo-mah fah-kuh
fork	um garfo	ooñ gar-foo
spoon	uma colher	oo-muh kool-yair
plate	um prato	ooñ prah-too
breakfast	pequeno-almoço	pe-keh-noo-ahl-moh-soo
lunch	almoço	ahl-moh-soo
dinner	jantar	jan-tar
starter	entrada	en-trah-duh
main course	prato principal	prah-too prin-see-pahl'
dessert	sobremesa	soh-bre-meh-zuh
rare	mal passado	mahl' puh-sah-doo
medium	médio	meh-dee-oo
well done	bem passado	bayñ puh-sah-doo

Menu Decoder

açorda	uh-sor-duh	bread-based stew
açúcar	uh-soo-kuhr	sugar
água mineral	ah-gwuh mee-ne-rahl'	mineral water
alho	ahl'-yoo	garlic
amêijoas	uh-may-joo-ush	clams
arroz	uh-rohsh	rice
assado	uh-sah-doo	baked
atum	uh-tooñ	tuna
azeitonas	uh-zay-toh-nash	olives
bacalhau	buh-kuh-lyow	dried, salted cod
batatas	buh-tah-tash	potatoes
batatas fritas	buh-tah-tash free-tash	french fries
bica	bee-kuh	espresso
bife	beef	steak
bolo	boh-loo	cake
café	kuh-feh	coffee
caranguejo	kuh-rañ gay-yoo	crab
carne	karn'	meat
cebola	se-boh-luh	onion
cerveja	sehr-vay-juh	beer
chá	shah	tea
chouriço	shoh-ree-soo	red, spicy sausage
cogumelos	koo-goo-meh-loosh	mushrooms
cordeiro	kur-deh-roo	lamb
dourada	doh-rah-dah	sea bream
fiambre	fee-ambri	ham
frango	fran-goo	chicken
frito	free-too	fried
fruta	froo-tuh	fruit
gambas	gam-bash	prawns
gelado	je-lah-doo	ice cream
gelo	jeh-loo	ice
grelhado	grel-yah-doo	grilled
leite	layt'	milk
manteiga	mañ-tay-guh	butter
mariscos	muh-reesh-koosh	seafood
ostras	osh-trash	oysters
ovos	oh-voosh	eggs
pão	powñ	bread
pastel	pash-tehl'	cake
peixe	paysh'	fish
pimenta	pee-men-tuh	pepper
porco	por-coo	pork
queijo	kay-joo	cheese
sal	sahl'	salt
salada	suh-lah-duh	salad
salsichas	sahl-see-shash	sausages
sopa	soh-puh	soup
sumo	soo-moo	juice
tomate	too-maht'	tomato
vinho branco	veen-yoo brañ-koo	white wine
vinho tinto	veen-yoo teen-too	red wine
vitela	vee-teh-luh	veal

Numbers

0	zero	zeh-roo
1	um	ooñ
2	dois	doysh
3	três	tresh
4	quatro	kwa-troo
5	cinco	seeñ-koo
6	seis	saysh
7	sete	set'
8	oito	oy-too
9	nove	nov'
10	dez	de-esh
11	onze	oñz'
12	doze	doz'
13	treze	trez'
14	catorze	ka-torz'
15	quinze	keeñz'
16	dezasseis	de-zuh-saysh
17	dezassete	de-zuh-set'
18	dezoito	de-zoy-too
19	dezanove	de-zuh-nov'
20	vinte	veent'
21	vinte e um	veen-tee-ooñ
30	trinta	treeñ-tuh
40	quarenta	kwa-ren-tuh
50	cinquenta	seen-kwen-tuh
60	sessenta	se-sen-tuh
70	setenta	se-ten-tuh
80	oitenta	oy-ten-tuh
90	noventa	noo-ven-tuh
100	cem	sayñ
101	cento e um	sen-too-ee-ooñ
200	duzentos	doo-zen-toosh
500	quinhentos	kee-nyen-toosh
1,000	mil	meel'

Time

one minute	um minuto	ooñ ee-noo-too
one hour	uma hora	oo-muh oh-ruh
half an hour	meia-hora	may-uh oh-ruh
Monday	segunda-feira	se-goon-duh-fay-ruh
Tuesday	terça-feira	ter-sa-fay-ruh
Wednesday	quarta-feira	kwar-ta-fay-ruh
Thursday	quinta-feira	keen-ta-fay-ruh
Friday	sexta-feira	say-shta-fay-ruh
Saturday	sábado	sah-ba-too
Sunday	domingo	doo-meeñ-goo

Selected Index of Places